COLLATERAL DAMAGE

Copyright © 2018 Glass Lyre Press
Paperback ISBN: 978-1-941783-54-2

All rights reserved: except for the purpose of quoting brief passages for review, no part of this book may be reproduced or transmitted in any form or by any means, electronic or mechanical, including photocopying, recording, or by any information storage and retrieval system, without permission in writing from the publisher.

Front cover art: © Tracy McQueen
Editor: Ami Kaye
Design & layout: Steven Asmussen
Copyediting: Linda E. Kim and Karen Bowles

Glass Lyre Press, LLC
P.O. Box 2693
Glenview, IL 60025
www.GlassLyrePress.com

Collateral Damage

A Pirene's Fountain Anthology

Glass Lyre Press

Contents

Margo Berdeshevsky
    Postcards To The Body Politic—   1
    Those Are Pearls That Were His Eyes. Look!   3

Carl Boon
    Berkin Elvan   5

Mara Buck
    Blood on the Street   6

Fern G.Z. Carr
    Lockdown – This Is Not a Drill   7

Joan Colby
    Dorothy   9

J.P. Dancing Bear
    The Oracle of Tender Shelters   10
    Dear Jeff   11

Carole Conner Davis
    Battered   12

Terri Kirby Erickson
    The Cost of War   13

Tikvah Feinstein
    Caterpillars & Bombs for Recess 14

Mike Finley
    Jacob the Crow 16

Susan Fox
    An Interdiction Forbidding Mourning: Tehran, 2009 18
    Cradle Song for a Child of War: Gaza, 2014 19

Diane Frank
    That Las Vegas Concert 20

Marc Frazier
    Bulletproof Blanket for Kids 23
    Human Declaration for the
    Return of the Children 24

Jessica Goody
    Radium Girls 25

Hedy Habra
    No Man's Land 26
    To Amal *(Because your name means hope)* 27

Vernita Hall
    Handcrafted 29

Lou Ella Hickman
    Vigil 30

Lois P. Jones
    After the Sniper 31

Allison Joseph
    Guilty 32

Laura M Kaminski
    Beyond the Facts: Sweet Sugar 33

Catherine Keefe
> What the Grandmothers Say 35
> Collateral Domesticus 37

Christopher Knodel
> Break Bread with Me, Brother 39

Rustin Larson
> Syrian Girl Crossing the Border from Greece 40

Lyn Lifshin
> Drawings of Children who got to the Thai-Cambodian Border 41
> Getting the Goods 42
> When the Borders Close 44
> Who Held the Camera so Steadily, and Why? 45

Alison Luterman
> The New Breed 46

Dennis Maloney
> Children's Drawings 48

Catherine McGuire
> For the Forgotten 49

Ken Meisel
> Child of the Moon 50
> Tamika's Eyes 53

Megan Merchant
> Swarm-Mind 56
> My father is concerned 58

Marsha Warren Mittman
> Scavengers (Northern India) 59

Cameron Morse
> Reading the Rain 60

Travis Mossotti
    These Resolutions   61

Robbi Nester
    Sandy Hook   63

Aimee Nezhukumatathil
    Two Moths   64

Connie Post
    Accessory After the Fact   66
    For All of Us Who   67

George Jisho Robertson
    III – A Petal In Fall   68

Michael Rothenberg
    Dead Kids   69

Neil Silberblatt
    Middle East Tautology   71

Kalpna Singh-Chitnis
    Kashmir   72

Amy Small-McKinney
    Open A Window   75

LeRoy Sorenson
    Getting Over It   76

Margo Taft Stever
    Nothing's Holding Up Nothing   77

Ambika Talwar
    Tangled Roots   78

Susan Tepper
    Boys   81

Jon Tribble
> The Drowned Boy   82

Maja Trochimczyk
> Standing Guard   84

Robert Walton
> One Percent   85

Martin Willitts, Jr.
> Little Gardeners   86

Kath Abela Wilson
> inland with water   96

Acknowledgments   99

Contributor Notes   101

Postcards To The Body Politic—

Margo Berdeshevsky

i

But there's more. First, I cannot write *dear*. I cannot call you *dear*. Am too deeply, deeply — and I have never believed in. Before. But now so much less. No. So much less. Dear illusion of *dear*. Dear I-could-not-write. You will not mind. You do not love.

Dear body. Dear *if-my-right-hand.* Dear how can you love only your own soul? Dear why would you feed only one eye? Not the hand. Not the belly. How can you love the head, not skin, not the water?

You make me cry. You make me sadder than women, sadder than men, even sadder than your —No. You, and your guns. Do you even love your hands? Can you love your mind? Body dangerous. I try to call you dear. Enraged at your arms, enraged at your desire, enraged at your eyes. If I am too angry to love you — what, what will we do?

ii

If a body meet a body. Where the body of the state falls. Or, because what not-to-be-trusted gods— refuse to fall. ...*twirling on the horse, blowing kisses— indefinitely into the grey future, and if this entertainment were to continue.* Body politic: How can I trust you? Fall. Because, I say: blind. Because the vulture can. Because the words of my mouth. Because if my hand offend me. Because if my diseased or broken— needs no teaching. All night, only the fallen wind. A breeze that needs no visa. A country to not belong to. Because I want — not to die. Because—us— or not at all. You make me cry.

iii

Just ahead of sleep. Soul to child-flesh on her sheet—like that frighten-me drop from— as if by falling— to reach the world. If the body meet a body. Teach me blood, and water. Every shell. Nested voices, I say, kicking open. Torn, from too much believing— cut out my swelling tongue. If I torture. If my right hand offend. Or my left. If my peace-cell be broken— let me be no human. Heartbeat. And skeleton. Please. Please. Teach me.

iv

If some child of an un-ended time— is also my "I." If some deviate boy of an evil-flower-mind. If savage-souled, and peace-broken. *Blowing kisses—Whip-cracking boss twirling on the horse— Tireless spectators by a merciless— A tottering mount in front of— Round and round the ring on— If some frail consumptive equestrienne were—*[1] Some god, I say: If no such country. If ashamed. If I choose to belong to none. Because the wind needs no passport. Wants none. Some god, I say: Don't you know an old or a new tongue? Can't you teach me a country that cannot lie? Bruised lips—un-sewn: what nest of voices sings in its shell in the groaning birch between thorn trees?

v

To be *saying*— *if you do not love me I shall not be loved   if I do not love you I shall not love*[2]. To be the left-hand cupped with "please" or belly, or spleen, or hope-hungry jealous of all the good I'm not —stopped. Just ahead of sleep, to child-flesh on her sheet— like that frighten-me drop from soul as if by falling— to reach the world and body   Or

With so much need. With such desire.

―――――   ~
1 *Franz Kafka / In the Gallery*
2 *Samuel Beckett / Cascando*

Those Are Pearls That Were His Eyes. Look!

Margo Berdeshevsky

Zealous for that seed, a word that might erupt in springtime.
Yearning for lightening. Un-painting midnight.
X might mark a spot for such a one, may his name be written,
    may it replace the dead, one fierce word — of grace—.
Wednesday's child full of grace, be born before we surrender to this
    nation.
Vagrant idea:
    One
Un-maker of America's pall, one, to turn rivers of blood back to water.
Those are pearls that were his eyes ...[1]
Such a one. A resistant? A candidate? A newborn? A warrior?
    Another blood-lost corpse?
Reorder the page of names, sequence reversed and replaced.
Quell the gun and its iron hands, the Congress and its glutton corpus:
    Child, child, child, be born!
Parents, can you sleep? Promise to turn a nation's vile tide to retreat.
Or who among us will imagine one child who did not die on
    Wednesday?
    Whose child turns in her sleep?
Nation of white hoods and guns and wars and true believers,
Murderers, and each willing servant of — a —
Lost-promise-soul.
    Nation of —
Killing and its men's game. Rotted with its blind-bullets-shame, its
Jewels that were their sight, fractured by a faux list of pride.
Instead, name after name of no child's
Holy open eyes, spoken. Backwards, as an inverted alphabet.
    None will
Grow tall, now — no blood flows backwards to a body shot. And stilled.
Fractured abecedarium characters that start a name: All will fail.
    None will rise.

Each or any name on the spoken page, will remain. Not rules or any of
    the
Dead. Not theirs—Not ours—can. Not now. Not each.
    Not any,
Carved by bullets into each descent of their breaths.
Bathe the bodies, close the eyes, bury their bloods — as though
    the sequence of an alphabet or a life might be reversed.
Against the rules. As Though The Sequence of An Alphabet Could—

an abecedarium, broken, in reverse, dedicated to the children alive and dead, in Parkland, Florida.

---

1 *Those are pearls that were his eyes. Look!*
— William Shakespeare, Ariel's song in The Tempest

BERKIN ELVAN

CARL BOON

One Sunday morning during the height of the Gezi Park protests in Turkey in 2013, thirteen-year-old Berkin Elvan of Istanbul was struck on the head by an errant tear-gas canister while walking from his home to a nearby market to buy bread. After nine months in a coma, he died on March 11, 2014. (From the Berkin Elvan Trilogy)

Six weeks' coma for the crime of no bread,
I watch your mother cry.

You can't hear her, see her, but her tears
are heavier than the canister of gas

that felled you, for the crime of no bread.
That keep you down, deaf to this,

blind to the tear-gas, the people screaming
because you can't. Six weeks. Six weeks

in the dark we share. If they call you a criminal
one day, we all are. If you die one night,

we all shall, carrying bread as light as air,
in hopes our mothers have such courage.

Past your vague and coma-bound dreams
a siren squeals among the buildings

in Taksim and a woman lies down
on the sidewalk to save you. I hear the call

to prayer break now across your city,
our city, where healthy men break bread

with soiled fingers. And hundreds gather still.
The bakeries must be open.

Blood on the Street

Mara Buck

We lose the names.
They disappear into non-memory with the softness of snow-melt.
Today they are the news,
the discussions at the water-coolers,
the texts on millions of phones, the social media squabbles.
The funeral flowers wilt and we go on—
until the next innocent is gunned down.

We lose the names,
because to retain them,
to take them out and savor them,
to dwell upon the pain and the suffering and the heartache
is too much for us to bear.
We prick our collective fingers on the thorns of roses,
and we suck the blood unthinkingly
like the vampire media whom we condemn,
but like them, we eavesdrop.

We lose the names.
The list is long, twining like a Hydra until it clutches us too,
until one of us or one of ours becomes a name fated to disappear,
even as we ourselves can't breathe.
Skittles and baby clothes,
textbooks and wedding invitations fade as dreams,
ephemera scattered
upon the welcoming asphalt.

Lockdown – This Is Not a Drill

Fern G.Z. Carr

Attention. Your attention please.
We are in lockdown mode.
We are in lockdown mode,

the intercom crackled
inside a portable classroom
occupied by twenty-five Grade 7's,
their substitute teacher and

                a broken door lock

Lights off! Metal shutters closed!
Under your desks! No talking!

silence,
total darkness
except for the flickering
of fluorescent-blue lights
as little fingers typed
terse text messages on their cell phones

              while they huddled under desks

another crackle: *The police*
have instructed the School Superintendent
to lock down all schools in the area.
This is not a drill; we don't know what's wrong.
Sit tight. Don't leave.

              the door might not be locked

an hour later, sketchy internet updates:
an incident –
one person shot in the face,
another in the back;
gunman still at large

        door lock still broken

students squirming
in blackness bruised
by flickers of fluorescent-blue,
muted whispers,
hunger pangs,
thoughts of bathrooms
and bullets

      suspect still at large

                                    broken lock

Dorothy

Joan Colby

They picked her out when the orphan train stopped.
She looked like a worker, a stocky girl,
Strong and solid. How wrong
They were. She went about singing,
Forgetting to feed the fowls
Or milk the cows. She burned
The bread and then the dreams
She persisted in telling. Silk hearts,
Cotton brains, wizards and such.
Lands sakes. She thought monkeys
Could fly. What's to be done
With such a girl. Then she ran off.
Just as well. It wasn't working
Out the way they'd thought.
But she came back to that wind-riven house,
That treeless prairie, the grey pair
With their puzzled, disapproving faces
And she told them there are witches
And silver shoes and a man
Who'd turned to tin and a lion.
And then she sang and sang and sang
Until the whole sky
Darkened.

The Oracle of Tender Shelters

J.P. Dancing Bear

Here is where humanity hums loudest
like an engine of discontent
no matter how much effort is made
to bury this place—
to make it hide.

Here each voice is a siren
calling out across the world to mothers,
mothers and their instinctive hearts—
mothers of the borderless regions
of emotion, mothers who are sirens themselves.

Mothers hear every note of music
and are boundless in their actions,

they are proud of whom they are, they are
citizens in a nation that expands
with every birth.

They hear an anthem play out in every child—
They hear the voice of Nature,
the endless voice of the universe
in every baby, hidden or known.

They look at the tiny borders of men
cutting the land, separating, dividing—
their little hands

trying to control, dominate, drown out, choke
the bonds of family. They love
to hate love. These men love
to hate women. And their children.
These small men, who have forgotten
their own childhood.

These men who have forgotten mothers.

Dear Jeff

J.P. Dancing Bear

When you smile your Loki smile, I see
them, you know—all those broken children
in your cages. People whose ancestors came
down through this land following the migratory animal
spirits, while your ancestors were a world away.
In that grimacing grin of yours, Jeff, the untreated
pox-ridden children are weeping and you wear
your bloody executioner's mask, harvesting
the asylum seekers, people so scared
of their deaths in their own countries
that your torture is still a better choice.
What is it about the poor and powerless
that makes you smile like that?
A death-head's grin—do you watch
as they suffer? Are you watching now?
When you tell your lies on TV, do you see
the dying? When I see you coyote
into Congress and claim you can't recall,
are you replaying the dust-choked children
who are crying for their mothers?
Jeff, tell me what the pharoahs sounded like
when they laughed in that bible of yours. Or
what tone the Devil took with Jesus
in the desert? People always assign too much
gravitas to the fallen angel's voice, where I
imagine your voice—a bit ephemeral and effeminate—
insisting within that good book of yours
the cruelty you inflict on the innocent
is something Christ would do.
Jeff, tonight thousands of people are wailing
in your cages, while the guards threaten
and menace in your name, in my name,
in the name of an America I wish you'd never
been born in.

Battered

Carole Conner Davis

His anger looms low in the room, a tornado set to
drop when conditions are right. The accustomed
pressure builds, our breath held awaiting touch
down, an abruptly striking eagle swoops
earthward to snatch its prey. Debris tossed in
all directions, gruesome sounds raise goose
bumps. Electricity coursing through a
torture chamber, we cower, swiftly
scrambling for shelter, or stand
shuddering cemented by fear
till violence plays itself out
and bitter winds retreat.
The impact haunts us,
bruised and misty-eyed,
our eventual return to
tranquility spent
sifting through
pieces of
destroyed trust,
wondering
what woes
our futures
face, as
lightning
strikes
the same
place
often
in
our

little
part
of
the
world.

The Cost of War

Terri Kirby Erickson

Like flocks of birds, children gather between
the burned-out buildings, the hollowed husks
of homes and schools and hospitals that rise
from the ground like rotting teeth in the mouths
of monsters. Nothing keeps them from coming—
not even bombs blooming in the distance like
blossoms made of dust and debris, fouling the
air and blotting out the sun. They find a stick,
a ball, a song that needs to be sung, a game in
the midst of wreckage and ruin, the echoes of
their laughter bouncing off the hardened hearts
of warmongers and power players—men and
women who will win and lose, again and again,
the same scorched earth beneath the children's
bare feet. But the little ones are learning even
now, who the leaders are, the followers, who
cries at the first blow, which child endures. The
dark shadow of adulthood falls early across their
dirt-streaked faces, their whippet-thin bodies—
because there is no such thing anymore, as play.

Caterpillars & Bombs for Recess

Tikvah Feinstein

There were black spotted caterpillars everywhere that spring. Like an invasion of tiny terrorists, their spiky bodies were dropping from trees, crawling over sidewalks and lawns. No avoiding the grossness of some being squashed by walkers on the sidewalks when I am assigned by the school nurse to guard the elementary school children during outdoor recess.

While we are outside, due to a bomb threat, the doors are locked as a precaution. I am watching from a bench, carrying icepacks, band-aids and tissues, a child's emergency injection for bee sting. The sun is warm, but the breeze is cool.

A multitude of the bugs are roaming in groups around the playground. A third grade boy, wearing a strange expression, has been sitting alone digging in the loose dirt beside the fence.

Three fourth grade girls have chosen some of the fuzzy creatures. They use pencil boxes to house them, and pick new green Sumac leaves to provide food. They show me these 'pets' with pride at their nurturing skills, but I remember the leaves can cause itchy rashes. It is already done. It would probably be best to have them wash up, but we are all together in the playground trying to stay safe during a bomb threat. I can't leave and I can't let the girls by themselves. I'm considering risks of an itchy rash as compared to a bomber on the loose.

I fix a bloody nose, a few scraped elbows and knees and give out an icepack. I feel disturbed by the lone boy with the strange expression, so I check on him. He's sitting legs stretched out on the ground around a pile of loose dirt watching a caterpillar he had buried attempt to escape out of the dirt, all the while piling more dirt on the insect. What he'd been doing since we'd been outside. The boy had been enjoying himself, and he didn't hide it. "No," I tell him. "That's not okay."

"I just wanted to see what it would do," he explained, as I picked up the caterpillar and placed it in the grass. "That's a living thing with feelings," I scolded, and made him stop. His expression was blank as he brushed the dirt off his pants.

When recess was over that day and we were safely let back in the school, I was so glad to hand the kids over to their teachers.

The next day, the girls came to school with rashes on their faces and hands that it hurt me to see.

I have come to regret that we are all losing our cherished freedoms while trying to keep safe. But I could not explain except to remind the girls from now on to avoid those poisonous trees. They soon recovered.

I think about the girls when I see the flaming Sumacs. When I see a caterpillar, I wonder about the boy, about the uncertainty that's come into all our lives. And say a prayer.

Jacob the Crow

Mike Finley

Down by the river the crows are calling in the cold.
Some have a metallic sound like a clang,
Others sound pinched as if the call
Is squeezed out from inside, like paste,
And coughing out the last dab that is in them.

Just now I hear a sound that jerks me around,
The hairs stand spike upright on my neck.
It is the sound of a boy calling out, *Ahhh!*
The voice vibrates as if running downhill,
And the sound bounds out of him that way,
Every thump a reverberating *Ah!*
I expect to see him waving a mitten
From the knoll across the marsh.

But it is a crow, perched low in a maple.
It dips its beak, and calls again *Ah!*
And for a moment I believe the crow and boy are one,
And the crow is saying, I saw it all,
And I alone survived.

A boy of eleven, bursting from a screen door
And running to a field, past the creek that runs
Through there, and stomping wet-footed through familiar places,
A journey that ends in a sack in the dark
in the trunk of a car in the bearded black spruce.

But when the man opens the lid the bag is empty
And the boy is gone, he was ushered away,
Installed alive in the topmost branches.
When people cluster like clucks at the scene
the black angels circling above mock their sorrow -
Why seek him here, the boy is flown.

And the eyes that adored every wild thing
Are different now, they do not blink,
The mouth never yawns, the limbs do not
Stretch out in bed at night like a song of skin
And humming blood and growing bone.

He who begged to be set loose was.
And now it is he who alights on the highway at dawn,
Stripping muscle from the runover body.
The other birds bray
About shiny tidbits fetched in the light of day,
They thrive like men on predictable dreams.

But behind the dull black bead of eye
Is a boy who knew darkness deeper than a well,
And cold more pitiless than snow,
Who knows the heart endures
What winter cannot kill,
And blinks.

An Interdiction Forbidding Mourning: Tehran, 2009

Susan Fox
for Neda Sultan Agha, shot by a sniper for not wearing a chador

The voice of Neda
her black hair
the white of her eyes
the black of her eyes
rolling, fixed
the black of her blood.

Decree:
no tomb, no forty days
of mourning rites,
no wailing, no outrage,
only the black of chadors
limp with unseen tears.

Chador: mask, sop,
tent of all forbidden grief:
cauldron in the hundred-ten degrees
of Tehran's summer:

Oh let the tears of one girl's murder
compress – in chador, in cauldron –
to steam,
to engine of unbanishable rage.

Cradle Song for a Child of War: Gaza, 2014

Susan Fox

Earth isn't still, my son
it turns
it rocks you
    not my arms.

Wood was alive that houses you,
my last-born joy.
It budded and greened
it teemed.
The woodpecker knew
the carpenter understood:
wood hacked and razed
breathes still
in earth that turns.

Wounds live, my infant love
though blood has fled
and slain flesh never scars.
Your wishbone ribs. Your emptied heart.
Your first words clotted in your throat
that once I kissed
and you laughed
and now no laugh
no cry
but still the wounds of your murdered flesh
work and will be heard.

I hold you still my buried boy.
Sands shift to the tides
tides roll to the moon
wood teems
wounds live
earth cradles as it turns
    my empty arms.

That Las Vegas Concert

Diane Frank
for Naia

What is the velocity of a bullet?
The trajectory of lives
at a concert for young fans
of country rock stars?
And if that old man wanted to leave this world,
why did he have to take
a trainload of children with him?

She ran to the stage and hid in the packing case
of a concert speaker
to escape the barrage of bullets.
Someone told her to run,
thought the shooter was headed for the stage,
but the information was wrong.
It turned her into a fish in a barrel,
an ant under a foot,
a girl with three bullets in her arm.

What is the velocity of light?
In a rocket, it looks like the speed of light.
An observer can be surprised
by formulas and calculations they don't understand.
Keep running. Keep running.

An off duty fireman
took off his belt to make a tourniquet
and kept her from bleeding out.
As she started to fall asleep,
he tapped on her chest and said,
Stay with me.
You're not doing to die today.

Shine a flashlight into the world,
into the dark night.
Breathe into the humming,
where the sun has become empty,
dreaming of rocks, planets, a young girl.

Time freezes and life
starts rushing back.
The fireman lifts her over a wall,
into a car, to the hospital.
Triage surgery,
three bullets removed from her arm.

Information is coming from too many directions.
Time becomes longer. Clocks are slower
between world lines.
Prayer for black holes
swallowing rifles in spacetime.

Now, mysterious music carrying
the voice of a thousand prayers,
calling you back to the world again.

Ignore everything you've heard
about observers affecting reality.
Bullets. Electromagnetism. The speed of light.
The force lines of shrapnel
reshaping her hand.
And what does this do to my world
where it isn't safe to listen to music?

Ten weeks later,
a young woman walks back
into the classroom where she teaches young children.
Her students stand up and cheer.
She doesn't tell them about the alarm on her door.
She doesn't tell them what she dreams at night.

If I step outside of the world,
I can see the curve of the planet.
You have to step outside of things
to measure them.
Her smile. The smile of time.

Life is a fortune cookie,
a flashlight shining into the emptiness,
gravitational waves from black holes,
a rocket careening
close to the speed of light.

The task ahead –
to stitch time back together.

Bulletproof Blanket for Kids

Marc Frazier
erasure from Business Insider article by Caroline Moss

It's come to this
shield small children from gunfire

by a company called ProTecht
5/16-inch pad

materials by our military
kids gunned down in 1st grade classrooms

arm your children with shields
you'll sleep easier at night

a quick, simple solution
maximum protection

any location
expect to be shot anywhere

bulletproof nap mats for tiny children
a sign we've given up

Human Declaration for the Return of the Children

Marc Frazier
from blind translation of Marjorie Agosin's poem:
Declaración humana par los derechos del niño

We all know the children
who have disappeared to mirror the earth
a vineyard of violet color
o like a ray of joy
the sky their best-loved turtle
upside down

We all know children who have disappeared
with the sway of the moon
with the weight of a canopy of green guavas
We all know the children
who have disappeared from milk
from chocolate to abandon their aunts

We all know the children who are gone
from the memory of corn
from the tempo of their cradles
dancers who descend and bend
We all know the children
who have disappeared
from their books the furry bears
that held them the alphabet from love
to the silence of the authorities

We all know the children
who have disappeared
from peace and left to war
gathered innocents
each alone a flawless gem
a hand that gives and not takes
We all know the children
hidden jewels blooming stars
fast dancing through pathways to the sky

Radium Girls

Jessica Goody

Watch dials gleam like abalone
with a phosphorescent glow.
Tongues flick over paintbrushes like lollipops.
Every flash of tongue delivers a steady dose;
the poison fills the veins like chlorophyll,
illuminating in the bloodstream
with a night-light's eerie glow.

Fingernails glint like blue-green algae
from the poisonous manicure,
transforming the expendable immigrants
into starlets with shimmering eyelids,
luminous mermaids and sparkling butterflies.

Strands of blood mix with the froth
of saliva and tooth powder,
vividly red against shining porcelain;
bleeding gums stain pristine handkerchiefs
edged with lace or monograms.
Teeth crumble into plaster
bearing the bitter-breath smell of rotting bone.

Bones rendered glassy and brittle
crumble like sand with every stride,
the broken fragments the green-white of mold.
The truth is starkly lit, a golden shadow
silhouetted against the paper's gloss.
Watch faces resembling miniature moons
are time bombs ticking a death knell.

No Man's Land

Hedy Habra

She was gathering thyme
on the winding hills
of South Lebanon

Two bullets
pinned her
to a thorny bush

Instead of wings
she had her harvest
of thyme.

TO AMAL
(BECAUSE YOUR NAME MEANS HOPE)
Hedy Habra

How can one think of better
days when streets
swarm
with armed men,
their uniforms
changing
with
the drift of war
their faces the same,
their eyes, your son's eyes.

Amal, your name means hope,
yet years
go by, darkening
days with violent ink,
night's pulse
resounding
through splattered walls,
treacherous alleys.
And what's left
of your sweet name,
when deafened
by the sound of anger,

you dream you're lost in Beirut's
neighborhoods,
in search
of a way home
in the midst
of rubble,
faceless gunmen

check your ID
for a Cross or a Crescent,
at every intersection.

Unable to withhold your boy's finger
from the trigger,
you lie,
your nightmare, a faint echo
of raging battles.

Handcrafted

Vernita Hall

The fabric of a child well-woven holds
no dropped stitches, interfaced by
father, mother, home, the family
All edges tightly bound with four-ply thread,
a richly patterned, storied tapestry

Families   fractured
separate;   kids cast-off
are pushed   by parents
together   like
chess   pawns, sewn
pieces   in patchwork quilts

Foster children
weaving in   and out
used   thread   bare
unr a v e l   q u i c k   B u t

      o   n   c   e   u n w o u n d

w o n t b i n d w o n t e v e r m e n   d a g a i n

              d
              o
              n
               t
            f
            i
           t

Vigil

Lou Ella Hickman

your child's body stretches out on your lap   a pietá

   as you remove the thorned crown of thoughts and prayers

                blood slowly crawls down the leg of your chair

   then drop by drop marks your vigil on the floor

        visitors pass   your silence answers their questions

      the outside darkness fills the window pane

      the Senator's secretary says

          i have to lock up now

    you reply

          i'll be back tomorrow

After the Sniper

Lois P. Jones

you came to the conclusion
a story must be told backwards
Once at the well of her throat

amethyst beads on the carpet
her palm flat against the floor
Embers in the last darkening

plum burnt and ash heavy
A pomegranate not yet split
with a knife

The curtain closed
after a season of bullets
One burst through

the frosted glass
knocking out a tooth
How she slumped

behind the lace drape
and its white
eyelashes   Her salt

still glistening on the brow
Of this   a day where
the sun rose as a fig

of untouched juices
Her book open to a page
of wild irises bent over

a canal of saints -
two lovers   making
whatever they could

GUILTY

ALLISON JOSEPH

You smack her face then kiss it well,
then make her swear she'll never tell—
she tells her boss some clumsy lie
about the welt beneath her eye,
a lump that didn't cease to swell

with your apology. She fell,
you claim to those who ask. You quell
their doubts. When strangers pry,
you smack her face,

make sure that she will never spell
out truth to those who think it's hell
to live with you. You keep her shy,
too scared to speak. She'd rather die.
Her skin once smooth as caramel,
you smack her face.

Beyond the Facts: Sweet Sugar

Laura M Kaminski
A Memorial

soft flesh does not know where to stand
ignorant and innocent, it does not know
Tuesday is not the day to ride the
bicycle and ring the bell, not the day
to cheerfully offer to take the elder
neighbor's coin for her to the market
promising to bring her back the very
biggest pound of sugar that they have

later, your mother blames the bullet
your elder neighbor's grief and guilt
leave her inconsolable and silent—
prostrate on your grave she rubs rough
earth into her skin as if this surface pain,
this process of slow-flaying is penance from
which only death can free her, as if she
finds her living flesh intolerable now

your father, thin, tightens a belt
upon heavy cotton pants so loose they
barely touch his legs before they're
tugged tightly, clipped and zipped
laced into his boots—he does not
blame the bullet or the gun—he does
not even blame the man who, like him,
thin and tired, fired — fired without
seeing a young boy on a bicycle, a
handle-bar basket of sugar, sweet sugar

he goes to work, your father, he takes
his post against a post, he slowly pans
his weapon's barrel across his pie-wedge

field of fire—they have all, in silence,
in the way they spit their wet tobacco
in the dust, shared this silent creeping
nightmare, this fear that when the time
comes and they must take the shot, the
field will not be clear, that someone's
child—a child with a doll or dog or
ball, a child with the best and biggest pound
of sugar—will suddenly appear behind the
bumper of the target's SUV, will suddenly
ring the bicycle bell and enter heaven

do not think he does not grieve, this man
your father as he stands, eyes watering
from sweat-salt and dust—sometimes
he will blot them, one only one at a time
with the worn back of his hat, the damp,
damp hair revealed clings immobile to
his skull, and in the solitude of this busy
market street he thanks God privately for
mercy, offers gratitude that can't be
spoken, thanks God again for mercy, sweet
mercy, that it was not his bullet that strayed

all day he prays like this, watching the road

What the Grandmothers Say

Catherine Keefe

We —— better than this every
body belly-soft waiting to be gunned down,
swift hate speech so juicy it spits
is not even close to our best. We ——

not any kind of us. Stand up straight
or gay and everywhere between that light bent
spectrum. Be not our worst. Bust out
of skin, ripe fruit from sun-tough drought

bark, reach new green so fast we can't look
back. You know your open window. Your face,
our beloved world and its messy, tired, can be dream-
less people who one day forgot the easiest thing

to do is bake lemon bread from the blooming sour
in spite of it all, squeeze every cut-finger stinging
drip-juice from one bumpy ass rind, beat sugar, crumble
leavening like the old city falls. We crack in two

eggs, settle thin batter in flimsy foil. Wait
like we are making something new. Walk next
door, head up, arms stretching hope's scent
so strong the bees will follow and pass the gift.

Only to a stranger you've not yet spoken to,
the one you think is odd, so different you never
say hello. Say hello. Say, I see you wanting a warm
sweet thing that reminds you of a grandmother

from the middle of nowhere, who stood her ground
before she knew that might come to mean meanness
not kindness. Say here, let's break together. What
is the food of your grandmother? What's the song

she sang to promise you were safe in darkness?
Hum. Together know the grandmother is never,
ever wrong and no wrong comes easy after we share
sweet crumbs and song.

Collateral Domesticus

Catherine Keefe

In Idlib tonight
there is a man
on his knees. There —

a body,
small. Child.
Let's call that one —

piercing the firmament —
let's call her
Mother. See how

she measures dead
weight in Pietà arms
without the same

serenity. Darkness slickens
stone until it too slides
beneath bombs' proof—

How relentless gravity
spins a revolution one cheek-
curve of the globe

away, day reveals
a break. Nobody too,
this — Mother woman

on her knees,
holds her own
body to account.

Clatters dried lentils into
cast iron pot, chops brown
onions to simmer

soup for the widow next
door. Tugs lavender
for the one whose son

shattered his clavicle and ribs
yet lived. Can you muddle
enough mint from one pot

that flower softens to sweet tea
for all who pass this porch too
parched? By noon a rose

named Peace blooms
against crushed
thyme. All day

into the bleeding
horizon she squints
to unravel the faith

meager as string tangled
in the stuck kitchen
drawer. Not in Idlib

tonight, she who cannot
sleep. To keep one eye open
on the tremulous scale.

Break Bread with Me, Brother

Christopher Knodel

Break
bread with me, brother, all of my needs are filled.
I try not to smother, but faith in Man should
build.

Break
bread with me, brother, I have a little more.
It will please my mother, to know I helped
restore.

Break
bread with me, brother, I have enough to share.
Please do have another, the weary must
repair.

Break
bread with me, brother, I have naught else to lend.
We'll sit by each other, your hunger I can
mend.

Syrian Girl Crossing the Border from Greece

Rustin Larson

The road, as I recall, was a pitted moonscape of chalk.
They came in a rush the last time, stun grenades in hand.
True friends stab you in the front, they say. I remember, once, being chased
by a black dog, August, an inch of lime in my lungs.
I lost my doll down a steep ravine; father clutched my slender arm.
Times, down an embankment, there's an apple tree with dust-covered fruit;
tastes sweet to your mouth, your razor-edged teeth.
Judge things just like a market scale: so many corpses
on one side, the living on the other. Judge things,
every single ocean; the earth, this ball of string unravelling.

Drawings of Children who got to the Thai-Cambodian Border

Lyn Lifshin

before they drew water
buffalo, leaves and
things to eat, later

heads apart from
any bodies darkening
in the sun. Bones

near the gingko with
out leaves, blood,
animals in pieces

the trees dying.
Blood on bamboo,
whips, men

yoked like cattle
forced to line up,
march off the cliff

Getting the Goods

Lyn Lifshin

In recent months, according to reports from Thailand published in the Far Easter Economic Review, murdered infants have been used to transport heroin across the border from Thailand to Malaysia

A wind blowing
thru dark
elephant grass, a
blood sun over
the rice fields a man

holds an infant
underwater, black hair
snakes, the
child gurgles then
doesn't. A plastic
rattle

bobs on the water like a
head before the water
goes from blood to wet
bark
the child is slit

emptied out like a
trout or hen stuffed
taut
and plump with
small bags of heroin

and before the
moon is a pale grape
in the

musky night a woman
paid as well as the dead

child's mother will
wrap the corpse in a
shawl, hug it close
seeming to smooth
the damp

hair into place as if
snuggling a
sleeping baby,
getting the goods
over the border

When the Borders Close
Lyn Lifshin

people stow away,
slip through
black water
at night.
It is like a hike
through black
leaves, everyone
together
in a clump.
My parents had a
three year old baby girl.
Everyone was taking hold,
caring for each other.
Wet birch and maples.
Whispering
under a blood moon.
Then the Germans
ambush
as the boat pulls out:
the child
held by her blonde hair
a sneering tall
Gestapo, his knife
against
her wet face

Who Held the Camera so Steadily, and Why?

Lyn Lifshin

Photographs
at the Holocaust Museum:
In black and white a
naked girl, maybe six,
gripped by the neck
in the hands of a woman with
huge biceps.
A mentally disturbed girl shortly
before her murder.
Near the dangling girl is a
photo in summer— trees are
fully leafed, dark smoke pours
out of one building.
Down the hall
a young woman with glasses takes
aim at a man
kneeling
in front of a pit of bodies: the
pistol points at the neck so no
shattered bone
will fly his way

The New Breed

Alison Luterman
for Emma Gonzalez and the other student activists

I see her on TV, screaming into a microphone.
Her head is shaved and she is beautiful
and eighteen and her high school was just shot up,
she's had to walk by friends lying in their own blood,
her teacher bleeding out,
and she's my daughter, the one I never had,
and she's your daughter and everyone's daughter
and she's her own woman, in the fullness of her young fire,
calling bullshit on politicians who take money from the gun-makers.
Tears rain down her face but she doesn't stop shouting
she doesn't apologize she keeps calling them out,
all of them, all of us
who didn't do enough to stop this thing.
And you can see the gray faces of those
who have always held power
contort, utterly baffled
to face this new breed of young woman,
not silky, not compliant,
not caring if they call her a ten or a troll.
And she cries but she doesn't stop
yelling truth into the microphone,
though her voice is raw and shaking
and the Florida sun is molten brass.
I'm three thousand miles away, thinking how
Neruda said *The blood of the children*
ran through the streets
without fuss, like children's blood.
Only now she is, the young ones are
raising a fuss, shouting down the walls
of Jericho, and it's not that we road-weary elders
have been given the all-clear exactly,
but our shoulders do let down a little,

we breathe from a deeper place,
we say to each other,
Well, it looks like the baton
may be passing
to these next runners and they are
fleet as thought, fiery as stars,
and we take another breath
and say to each other, The baton
has been passed, and we set off
running hard behind them.

Children's Drawings

Dennis Maloney

The drawings are rough and crude
like those my son
or your daughter
brought home from school
full of awkward lines
and smudged colors.

Blue, green, red, yellow…
but unlike those drawings
of houses with oversized doors and windows,
with colorful rainbows & stick figures,
a bright yellow sun dominating the sky,
with children at play
in tree forts four stories high,
these are different.

These are drawings
of children caught in war.
Images of planes
and helicopters dropping bombs
on huts which burst
into orange-red flames
and soldiers in green
with machine guns and machetes
to kill the fleeing peasants,
slicing the heads of women
and written in shaky captions
'shut up you guerilla wives, we sharpen
our machetes for your heads.'

For the Forgotten

Catherine McGuire

With half-lives far shorter
and story lines tainted
with poisons anathemic
to Western hope and gumption,
the towns swept by earthquake
flood or fire continue
long past our fickle
spot of attention.
Small bodies like seaweed
washed up on the beaches.
Like comets, they drew us
the film clips, news columns
of breathless outpouring:
foodstuffs, used clothing
bandages, water —
once "safely" in refugee
camps, they're forgotten.
When did we last think of Haiti
New Orleans or Chili?
How long past disaster
does our focus linger?

Child of the Moon

Ken Meisel

Sweet child of the moon, I see you
Standing there alone on your front lawn,

Your chocolate popsicle in hand,
Your eyes, drooling up at me.

Your mother, alone on her couch,
The needle in her arm and your father

Alone in his cell, another tattoo
On his arm, your picture on his wall.

Do you see the radiant stars?
The fireflies so delicate, lighting up

The sunken shrubs? Do you see
Where the face across the moon

Is your sister, rising up for you,
And the stars, your brothers,

So many of them you cannot count?
Somewhere, beyond you,

Where the fires burn at dusk,
And the clouds dissolve in indigo,

And the windowless buildings
Of the city gather their olive glow,

You will find the crow flying
Noisily alone there, past you,

And you will follow him, past
Your mother and your father, past

The bridge stretching over the water
Where the moonlight is ochre

And the angel's trumpets, strangled
Into the trees, shout out your name.

And, when you hear it, your name,
Your heart will fill with it, your name,

And your blood will carry awe,
The first kiss of desire, and you will

Become the mystery to yourself, oh
Angel of representation, oh lonesome

Wolf-child who carries the heart
Of a deer inside the arms of a bear.

And you will be one of them who
Gathers varied shelters and departs;

Who leaves the angry drill tone of those
Who mangle the face, injure the heart;

Who loves because the eternal rests
Inside you, so vacant and emptied,

Your ribs, nothing else but silhouette
And the gable row of skin and nettles,

And your small face, a radiant moon-
Stone, your eyes, singing, igniting;

And then you will leave them, these
Broken starlings that are your parents,

This town so desolate and alone,
So baked in clam shells and pollution,

And you will rise up, full of music,
Your heart, spilled open, full of night.

Tamika's Eyes

Ken Meisel

Tamika's fourteen, and she's been raped
by a man in an alleyway, on a cardboard box,
under a sprawling maple tree that's gone yellow.
This is in Detroit, where nothing but violence,
mixed into the high clouds with factory smog
thundering across the wet sky in big rain squalls,
is left to remind us all who drive underneath it
that grief, which is the way the eyes catalogue pain,
comes forth in big spools of tears and woe.

Tamika tells me the story as we play crazy 8's.
It's strange, a girl of fourteen telling me a man's
sins back to me. Especially when she still
paints her finger nails pink and sleeps curled up
with a teddy bear in her bed. A girl shouldn't
have to tell a man's sins back to him,
but she tells me, and so I'm a part of her story.

This is also the year I learn that pain is contagious.
And, because I am still young, and I don't yet
know that pain is contagious and it disables
a part of you forever if you take it,
I take it from a girl telling me a man's story
back to me, and it disables me, and that's
why I am like this now. I have some of a girl's
damage inside of me. You know, it's as if I, too,
am infected with a part of this girl's life.
It's as if I, too, am blessed with this kind of luck.

I tell you, when Tamika cries, it's astonishing
what her face does, for she cries deeply,
like a kid in a mirror trying to find herself

from some sort of erasing that has happened to her.
Sometimes she cries herself into breathlessness,
and she has to grab her shoulders and slow down.
And her grief resembles a child awakening
from some kind of nightmare because it is wide-eyed
and astonished. It's full of her eye's heartbreak.

And when I look at how she cries, it's like she's
breaking the bloodied peat moss of her heart
across her own two hands—as an act of anguish
and sorrow against a violent event that's happened
to her little body, which is the only definition
of war I can think of that everyone believes,
because the body is the sacred symbol of the world
being torn asunder or cradled in safety…

~

I suppose it's true that a girl sized up by somebody
with a prize on his mind is a girl marked,
and what is left of the stars in her back pocket
that you think she ought to reach for,
well, they really amount to something as small
as crushed dollar store beads. And the little lamps
that are her eyes trying to see a world's
character flaws, or its snows of spring flowers
rising simultaneously together,
stay fixed in bewilderment forever, or else
she gouges out their future light
with the nervous tips of her fingers in the after-flow
of trauma and shame and self-woe,
and she's left blinded, just like a stunned angel,
she's a rabbit in the middle of a road
trying to crawl back to where things started.

But Tamika tells me she's glad we cried together.
She says, sometimes, all we can do is open
our eyes and cry, until all the hurt in there is gone.
And then she sits back, heaves a big round sigh.
And the noises of the city enter the room again.
We hold hands in silence, like old friends.

I figure we're all like conduits that conduct
each other's pain no matter what the casualties are,
no matter what the gains and losses will be…
Maybe that's why beauty and evil come together,
and the shared sexes have to deal with it.
And if we don't conduct it, I guess we're both just
lost, and either way we're both together,
either way we both carry the burden, and it stains
the one big quilt that is our shared life,
and that is the law of contagion that makes us.

~

When Tamika first sees me, she's at the top
of the stairway ready for bed, her teddy bear
tucked under her elbow. Her eyes are like steel…
Her fingers twirl a sharp yellow pencil,
as if she's waiting for one more man to attack.
When I say goodbye to Tamika for the last time
she tells me I'm like her uncle, even though
I'm white. Her eyes, though they're full of mist,
shine like tiny bright blinking light bulbs,
and she tells me she hopes she can get herself
back to into school in one safe piece.
It's as if she's ghosted in a mirror—
like she's waiting for something to get clear—
and if she is to find herself again in a man's eyes
and see herself better, she must find
someone to tell it to, and this time it was me.

Swarm-Mind

Megan Merchant

We agree that arsenic will rain down on a concert of dancers,
dropping them to the ground when it splashes into their sweat.

We agree it will be allowed into the food supply, packed into
lunchboxes of a kindergarten class. Bleed their tongues from the alphabet,

leave holes in the hand-sewn sweaters and songs. We agree it will
be buttered into the popcorn at a movie theatre, emergency exits sealed,

and packed into textbooks that say *the best minds of my generation did not
know how to stop this.* We agree it will happen again.

We agree so that we can hoard it in our cabinets and pantries, ruffled under
beds, in case the government should rise, or a man invade our home at dark.

How we would put the kettle on, sit him down and ask if he was
(abused, mentally ill, disgruntled, maltreated, angry)—ask why.

Then, here—Sip, it will soothe you. We will spoon it into the honey and serve.

We will save the day. And mourn the losses, the times arsenic was used
on (children, husbands, sisters, wives, teachers, lovers, and battered spouses),

we will rant for at least an hour. And then the lights will dim
and we will read our children to sleep with this myth of redemptive violence,

because it is the only story we have memorized. Handed down from generation
to what's thinly left of our future. And we will agree to call it arsenic

because it is close to toxic masculinity, but also close to the tart poison of monarchs,
and if this is our last stand, we will refuse to let what remains of beauty

be chewed through by bullets. We know how this will look to history.
So instead, we will say it was a wing, crumpled under our tongue, that kept us silent.

My father is concerned

Megan Merchant

my fourth-grade son isn't learning math, the proper way, the rote way, by memorizing tables, like he did as a child. A ruler to a wrist. Over and again. I tell him the nearest gun store is 2.3 miles from where my son is erasing a mistake, from where he is subtracting the number of bullets emptied in sixty seconds, minus how many times the heart beats in that frame, minus how many children can fill a supply closet. Then add how many days it takes for a parent to lose the sound of their child's voice from memory (Less than you think). My son, who is schooled in divergent thinking, recognizes x as a murder of crows, an unkindness of ravens—a funeral in the sky.

Scavengers (Northern India)

Marsha Warren Mittman

the mountains loom large
not pine laden and fragrant
nor craggy and awe inspiring
rather huge piles of garbage
that daily grow higher
foul, rotting, reeking
of human waste and remnants
and the women children
(small girls mostly since
young boys are conscripted
for menial labor tasks)
search and dig through
the odiferous malignant heaps
for any prize piece of cloth,
object, metal to sell or
worse, for a rotting morsel
to eat, starved as they are.
with blisters and open sores
on their hands and feet
where constant contact is made
and the seagulls, natural
scavengers of the trash,
fly about competing for food
the gulls ultimately having
the choice and ability to leave
but with no skills, money, education
the human scavengers, the untouchables,
are relegated to garbage for life

Reading the Rain

Cameron Morse

The thunderhead groans,
rolling down like a garage door
to pinch out the orange light of the horizon.

Last night's rain dampens
the pages of the newpaper flung
at sunrise. It waits for me to make my pilgrimage

to the foot of the driveway, for my socks
to soak up the blood of the latest gunshot victim.
Today it's a four-year-old boy

who slept through a drive-by, once,
for the rest of his life. It waits for me, for you,
for anyone, to scan the blank

page of heaven, and listen to the earth
gurgling below us.

These Resolutions

Travis Mossotti

...ex vita ita discedo tamquam ex hospitio, non tamquam e domo...
—Cicero, De Senectute

For a brief moment last night I felt myself wanting to
exercise with the fierce despondency
of a Hollywood darling prepping
for another hero role that demands him
shirtless in three scenes, but come morning
I ate a day old donut and wrote a poem instead
and felt much more like myself
suddenly than I had felt in years—
remembering how cold Steve Harvey looked
the night before as he hosted the New Year's Eve
bash in Times Square and waited for that glitzy-ass
disco ball to drop, and how warm
I was at home toasting my toes fireside
with my love; but beyond my impossible
albeit fleeting desire to possess the obliques
of Adonis, I watched the crowded streets
over the shoulders of the host and hoped,
in the way in which America has become
accustomed, to please let the night pass
without some lone shooter leaning the nose
of his hungry rifle over a railing
with all the cameras looking dumbly on.

And now, in this barely new year, I'm thinking
about what didn't happen, but does so often happen
that the image of the party's host applying
pressure to a bullet wound, as anno
domino edges us closer to the edge
of oblivion, seems plausible and almost,

dare I say, acceptable; and, since I'm being honest,
sometimes, after the surviving families
have been notified, bodies tallied for a news
ticker's endless coursing, my momentary

grief morphs into another flag draped over
any coffin, which is the founding of anything known.
There is a language where the word
for murder does not exist, but this universe,
which is assuredly finite, won't let us speak it,
and so our killing and resolving not to kill
have simply become how we measure
and balance; it's how I can say to my children,
after working for hours to piece together
Van Gogh's Starry Night from an old,
1000 piece box I've had since I was their age,
go to sleep now, it's late, we'll finish
the puzzle tomorrow, knowing that even
as the words escape my lips and turn
into a fledgling promise, there's more
than one piece missing from that box.

Sandy Hook

Robbi Nester

Goldenrod, cerulean, and teal.
Violet-blue and burnt sienna.
On every desk, boxes of 64
Crayola crayons, tall and straight
as soldiers. It's almost Christmas.
Decorations make the windows
glow. When the door swings open,
I expect a holiday surprise. Instead,
a boy in black, masked and hooded
like a ninja, steps in. Belts of bullets
stretch across his chest. No time
to cry, to run. The gun stares hard
with its one silver eye. This isn't
a movie, where the good guys
come. The teacher tries to
hide us, but bullets fly
so fast. Now she won't
wake up, no matter how
I shake her. No crayon
could ever be that red.

Two Moths

Aimee Nezhukumatathil

Some girls   on the other side of this planet

will never know   the loveliness

of walking   in a crepe silk sari.   Instead

they will spend   their days   on their backs

for a parade   of men   who could be   their uncles

in another life.   These girls memorize

each slight wobble   of fan blade as it cuts

through the stale   tea air and auto-rickshaw

exhaust   thick as egg curry.

Men   shove greasy rupees   at the door

for one hour   in a room

with a twelve-year-old.   One hour—   One hour—

One hour.   And if she cries afterward

her older sister will cover it up. Will rim

the waterline of her eyes with kohl pencil

until it looks like two silk moths

have stopped to rest on her exquisite face.

Accessory After the Fact

Connie Post

I destroy the evidence
upon waking
wash the blood
from bad dreams

I make sure there is no
subconscious spatter
on the curtains
the floor
the blankets are pulled
from the bed
washed over and over

I cover the mattress
with a loose sheet
hide the evidence
– the shards of night
I hope nobody notices
how I left my body
fled the crime scene

burned the dreams
with one lit match
the ashes of a single nocturne
falling out of my mouth

For All of Us Who

Connie Post

It was my brother, it was my uncle, I was alone, someone was in the next room, it was my father, I was young, I was in third grade, I was in college, I knew him, I didn't know him, he put something in my drink, I was wearing winter clothes, I wasn't wearing any clothes, I was on my way to work, I was on my way home, I was afraid of him, he told me he would fire me, he told me he would kill me, he told me to shut up or he'd take the kids, he told me I was a whore, he told me I teased him, he told me I would ruin the family, he told me no one would believe me, he said nothing and stared through me until I was dead, I didn't tell for years, I told and was not believed, I have never told, I have bad dreams, I avoid parties, I avoid dark rooms, I avoid long lurking glances, I avoid skirts, or winter or summer or seasons where my skin remembers violation. I drink, I don't eat, I keep it quiet, I tell my friends, I take pills, I don't walk alone at night, I hold my lover's hand, I worry too much about my kids, I need to tell the truth. I need to tell the truth. Please listen.

III – A Petal In Fall

George Jisho Robertson

Snagged on a rosebush

I taste blood salt

Beside the dark ocean of its own device

shore birds rise and fall. They call

'Brother, do you hear us?

Sister, will you follow us?

Take wing with us, take wing…'

Dead Kids

Michael Rothenberg

dead kids!
they are the collateral damage of the nra
collateral damage of the pharmaceutical companies
collateral damage of immigration policies
don't talk to me about pro-life
because that fetus you want to save today
will be sacrificed tomorrow to this gross
and violent experiment
in greed and hate

dead kids!
that's what we get everyday
that's what this country makes best
the new homegrown product
made in america!
a country in grieving

dead kids!
it makes me sick
the dead children
yes, we are angry snowflakes
and we will take you down…

dead kids!
shot dead in the street by racist cops
dead kids!
bombed to death on a beach in gaza
dead kids!
starved to death while the rich get fatter
dead kids!
drowning for diamonds to be worn on main st.
dead kids!

Burned to death in toxic bangladesh tanneries
dead kids!
we don't know how to stop it
but there will be more for everyone
when the kids are dead

dead kids!
they are the collateral damage of the military industrial complex
collateral damage of the prison industrial complex
collateral damage of the free enterprise capitalist pogrom
don't tell me about pro-life
because that fetus you want to save today
will be sacrificed tomorrow to
this sociopathic experiment
in greed and hate

dead kids!
shot dead in the street by racist cops
dead kids!
bombed to death on a beach in gaza
dead kids!
dead kids!
dead kids!
we don't know how to stop it.

july 27, 2018

Middle East Tautology

Neil Silberblatt

The friend of my enemy is my enemy.

The enemy of my enemy is my friend.

The friend of the enemy of my enemy is my friend (once removed).

The enemy of the enemy of my enemy is my foe, unless
he is also the enemy of the friend of my enemy.

The child of the friend of my enemy has not
yet declared sides.
Does not yet know that his brother is dead.
Hides under his bed
to dull the noise of nightmares
and mortar shells.

The blood of my enemy
and the friend of my enemy
and his child
is on my hands
and the hands of my enemy
and his friends.

Kashmir

Kalpna Singh-Chitnis

I

No one knows her here by her name,
the one, who is sitting mum
there, on a wooden log.

The woman whose son was slaughtered
with a chainsaw
is the only identity she has
in this refugee camp.

II

The night they fled their village
leaving behind their home, hearth
and half-cooked bread on the stove,
who had come to see them,
on a night before that night?

And why didn't they open their door
for anyone after that?

Even before they could tell us,
why they had not been able to look
into the eyes of their daughters
since then...

a Chinar[1] falls,
making a creaking sound,

---

[1] Chinar is a type of deciduous tree found in Kashmir, and other Himalayan regions. Its botanical name is Platanus orientalis.

they could never tell us all
what they really wanted to…!

III

They have in their memories their home,
and the only flower blooming
in their backyard,

and a cot left outside,
soaking in the pouring rain,
the night they fled.

They have in their memories
their dialogues, laughter,
and sweet sun;

and everything else,
that they could not bring along
with themselves;

and their little ones,
who did not return home,
after they went to play

soon after the day,
when the snow in the valley
had melted away.

IV

A little girl
playing outside her tent
did not come to us,
even though, we invited her a million times.
She darted back into her tent
and stood by the door,
holding the ropes tight
on both sides,

it is as if,
she wouldn't allow anyone
inside her home
anymore!

The faces she does not recognize,
those strangers
cannot trample
her new home.

Open A Window

Amy Small-McKinney

for air, notice the airlessness
of bodies piled up
like newspapers, the airlessness
of fear, not the kind you feel
on a mountain ledge when
you don't trust
your body's sense of balance,
rather the kind you can't imagine—
someone you never met
will kill— has planned to kill
for over a year, stockpiling ammunition
that will enter abdomen chest or head
as velocity from rifle barrel expressed in numbers
as v in meters per seconds
as the bullet departs its barrel
and velocity becomes zero,
as in that moment you become zero.
It has nothing to do with you.
It could be any number
of people unless you are standing there
in its general direction.
The shooter understands,
it is physics and math.

Getting Over It

LeRoy Sorenson

I've never gotten over northwest gales,
the reds and yellow of tulips, the paradise

of fall wheat. I have never gotten
over brother, parents, grandparents, aunts

and uncles, cousins and lovers dead
before I was forty. The stinging smell

of a woman's wet hair intrigues
me as does my best friend's search

to find the prime well of truth.
I don't believe in the clean break

from misery. I believe in regret, the stain
of history. I believe in shaking trees,

air sick and forlorn. I believe in the treason
of the heart. And my heart cleaved.

And the evil of the descending belt.

I believe in a language stripped
of all words but ache.

Nothing's Holding Up Nothing

Margo Taft Stever
El Salvador, 1982

Under the floorboards with the wood
rot, the insects, ants skittering to
and fro, the mother hides with her child.
Her nipple's in the infant's mouth,
but her milk won't let down.

She did nothing, but the officials
suspected, decided to make an example,
the child dragged out, beaten,
the bellies of flowers, blackened,
the bells, the bells,
the long toll of roots …

It is hard to believe anything
was ever alive under here, under
these boards, anything alive
for long under these boards.
Filaments break off and powder
as if they never were wood,
as if the hollows were roads
going somewhere, as if the mother's
breasts could fill with milk, as if
her child could breathe again.

Tangled Roots

Ambika Talwar

Stop this weeping, Child,
Your tears have drenched
a hungry river
where bones lie lifeless dry
almost ready
to fly....
From there behind *gulmohur*
I have watched you for weeks.
Child looked at Beggar in brown
shirt with *khakhi*
ribbons
dipped in almost red
in a violet sun-setting Sky.
Her dress a plumage of broken red
lifted a little in dusky wind,
her legs caked with red muddy.

Her breath was raspy
but voice clear
in mysterious wind kissed with soot.

I cannot be born any more, Child said.
My mother is gone,
my sisters laid to rest.

A brother who could have been
was seared in a war — of him nothing
remains. So I weep,
Child said,
before I disappear.

Sudden as a thrill a flock of wild hawks
shot up from nowhere
shattered Sky with shrieking.

Beggar looked up at the tearing Sky,
but not a drop of rain kissed our Earth.

Oh Child, he said, turning to her.
Frantic, She was busy gouging Earth
as a she-wolf might.
No-name Seed burnt-orange streaked
with umber
ochre emerald peered
lay wound amid old tangled roots.

Child wept while *Vayu*, wind god,
swallowed her sobs into silence.

She tore Seed out of root's clutches,
rubbed until it shone like a gaze. Seed fit
her palms like destiny.

She showed Beggar the gazillion lines on it
Broken vows – man's ignominy to land water air
this Seed, hollow-full with love's fire.

Beggar's eyes crowded with rain
his gown mud-redder torn.

She kissed Seed of a trillion stories.
Swallowing half, Child slowly
curled up like a baby

un-born
a Seed.

In her hand the other half Seed,
her hair full of dust.

Boys

Susan Tepper

All the boys are beautiful
but we don't know it
yet— we girls
spending hours on the phone
instead of homework
or watching the younger kids,
sweeping up the kitchen,
or taking out the trash

no— we talk and talk
tearing the boys to ribbons:
this one's freckles, this one's
knobby knees, the one
with sloping shoulders, another
too smart for his own good.

A decade or more goes by and
growing older, we wish we'd been
less critical, finished our homework,
done the dishes, acted kinder
toward these boys who grew up, too.
Going off to the war to die.

The Drowned Boy

Jon Tribble

Red and white, death's confection,
the ambulance packed away in its maw
still flesh—malleable and gray now
what was just hours ago elastic, brown,
vibrant, smiling twelve-year-old.

Trapped beneath the dock's creosote
pilings, his thrashing silent amidst
the other campers' loud midday swim,
the boy's struggles settled like
pine needles carpeting to the soft bottom.

His buddy with no one to clasp hands,
sing out with at next count, the life-
guards scanned the stilling water,
checked boathouse and empty bathrooms,
called names and counted again. But

he was gone. Counselors ran for help,
strong swimmers drew deep breaths and
dove into the lake's dull shadows,
retrieving branches like sodden flailing
arms from deep water, stones with now

the weight of hopes tossed from shallows.
Canoes and boats dragged beyond orange
buoys, eyes scouring shoreline, paddles
probing sunken logs and brush. Always
Kevin! Kevin! echoing back and forth,

a metronome keeping precious time while
tucked away beneath restless feet upon
the weathered planks above, the body
lost all that could answer, all shape
and sweep of life giving way to the water's

relentless murmur, slow wave of current
creeping into the fingers' unintended
flutter, the eyes' clouding gaze. When
they found him, the ambulance long since
had become a different kind of sentinel,

the searchers realizing the probabilities
of breath and heart, the power of lungs
and prayers. Still, as my father watched
the divers lift the corpse from the lake,
cradle it to the stretcher like porcelain,

like a bride or lover crossing a threshold,
—until the medics pulled the blankets up,
until they covered the pasty face—he knew
somehow the boy would be alive, somehow
this miracle would happen. But as the doors

closed, the gravel sprayed out in undeniable
retreat, my father, trembling, hid his face
in shaking hands and wept, echoing his sobs
over the lake and the white cross reflecting in
its mirror, offering no glimpse of redemption.

Standing Guard

Maja Trochimczyk

At a tombstone for strangers, she
shivers in the freezing rain of April.
A white shirt, pleated navy skirt, school sweater.
The longest hour. Red tie. An ugly beret.
Not allowed to move, sit, turn, frown,
or scratch her nose. Not allowed to
talk to the other girl. No smiling.
Eyes fixed, looking straight ahead.

The longest hour. This is how the dead
consume the living. Reverse cannibalism.
Would she have volunteered, had her parents
told her? Two great uncles, priests at Dachau:
One relieved of his ills in a gas chamber,
one liberated, with his body, spirit broken.
A Home Army fighter killed in Auschwitz.
Two others hanged in the Lublin Castle.

One survivor of Majdanek and Gross Rosen.
Three siblings from the Warsaw Uprising,
buried under ruins in September 1944.
Those who perished in the Soviet Gulag.
That officer shot in the Katyń forest.
The list goes on and on. Is that
what a ten-year-old should learn?

One Percent

Robert Walton

I am the pebble in your shoe,
The shifting shadow
In the alley,
The gleam of steel
In a stranger's hand,
The caustic gas
In babies' lungs,
The starved whimper
In a refugee's throat,
The flat, black clack
Of an AK's action,
The scarlet blossom
Of an improvised bomb;
I'm Somalia, Syria and Ukraine;
I'm Benghazi, Homs and Chicago.

I'm the pebble.

Little Gardeners

Martin Willitts, Jr.

During WW II, Eerde Castle near Ommen, Netherlands was used by Quakers to hide over 200 Jewish children (1934–41). The children described their accounts in "The Little Gardener's Album"

1.

(All wars are the same war —
only the efficiency of destruction
is different.)

2.

In spite of the circumstances
moldy bread is quite exceptional.
We grow our own vegetables
in spite of the blackouts.

In spite of the lack of rain,
we gather tears from the smaller children
into a watering can.

2.

Bombers thunder overhead.
We call them harmless mosquitos.

3.

Tomatoes are big as starvation eyes.
Tomatoes are juicy memories of home.
These circumstances are tiny victories.

We plant in survival
and in spite of the hindrances of squirrels
or fear.

It is good that the Quakers teach silence —
otherwise, we would make noise
waking combat boots.

      4.

In spite of distance
we can hear our parents dying.

      5.

Someone says the enemy is near here.
We shall greet them with laughter.
We shall show them our hands holding peppers,
and they will remark,
They are harmless little children.
They will never know where we had hid our gold stars.

We planted the stars in the garden.

At night, those stars are string beans heading into sky.
We want to climb them and place more stars
so everyone can see there is no difference
between one star and another.

6.

We wear out the ground with our knees
planting in soil.
The earth speaks a different language
than ours.

Although adults say things look grim,
we see the efforts of cucumbers
climbing the fence
as fingers.

7.

Someone says the school is seven years old.
My brother is the same age.
It is silly to think they have the same mother.
But when I see him
trying to grow into his britches
and his socks sag in angles
while he fights, uselessly, to straighten them,
I think, how careless this world
to allow adults to fight over nothing.

8.

When they captured our music teacher,
Billy Hilsey, to them it was another conquest.

He looked like a music sheet
as they took him to wherever he will vanish.
We are told never to speak his name again.

We are commanded
by the man wearing totally black leather.
His sidearm is as polished as his hip boots.
He clicks his heels when he is finished speaking.

He was addressing the houses in the village
as if they had ears. He told the houses,
if they saw anyone suspicious
to report to him immediately.

I wait for one of the houses to speak to him.
What exactly would a house say?
Would a house tell this man who to trust?
Would it confess it knows where we are hiding?
Will the doorknobs turn us in?

     9.

It is fashionable to hate.
Is it the same way in your part of the world?

Today, we talked about tolerance
and in the distance was shooting.

When I see myself in a mirror
is my face really so strange?

Children outside are holding hands
in a ring of silence, praying for love.

10.

On the radio we hear about cleansing this earth
of the undesirables. We know it is about us.
We are so small and the world is so large and angry.

They say we are a hindrance. Like a pebble
in a shoe. Like a toothache. Like dress rehearsals
for silence when night arrives as a march of boots.

They say, *Help is coming, sit tight, wait it out.*
We can hear trucks approaching, men inside
click bullets into chambers.

Someone said Billy Hilsley was shot at close range
for giving the wrong answer about supporting Jews;
someone said he escaped, disappeared into a dike.

Someone is whispering like a radish —
small and tortured, like candles blown out in hearts,
like castle walls ricocheting noises at night.

11.

Someone wants to rehearse a play, *As You Like It*.
How perfect to confront fear with laughter.
When the enemy approaches they will find Shakespeare.
We work on the production and design sets
and drape them with nosegays from the garden.
We take broccoli as trumpets to announce each scene.

12.   (Based on their actual plans, 1941)

Lately it has been hot.
Perhaps we have imagined the searchlight.
We are expecting thunderstorms
as humidity shifts its feet nervously.
We wilt like flowers in such glare.

We will have a procession through the garden
solemn as a gathering of woodchucks.
We shall have a party at 5 o'clock
when the evening cools off a little.

It will be a time of cake and coffee.
We have been hoarding these treats a long time.
It is hard to be patient when you are a child —
but hiding like this, pretending
we do not exist, keeping silence as a cloak
heavy with fear, is good practice.

We will decorate the tables with heliotropes
and pennants we made from torn scraps
fastened to lamps
we cannot light, for fear of exposure.

We made play called *"The Weeds Don't Die"*.
We will play the parts of weeds.
Nothing can kill them.
Not even the enemy.

We will sing until the rains arrive.
How delightful if the rains should join our singing.
Mrs Neurse will run outside to get her baby;
both of them will return drenched as puppies.
Wulf will have to rescue our booths
erected in front of the gate. All the throwing booths
will be soggy and droopy as lost laughter.

Along will come the saturated horse wagon
with Olga and Kurt Warschauer
pretending to be farmers.
Eventually everything will dry out.
Eventually we will have ice cream.
No one will dream of troubles this night.

        13.   September 1, 1941 – April 1, 1943

Our mood dried out when the army passed near.
Our Jewish teacher, Elisabeth Schmitt
is placed in charge of the remaining seventeen
Jewish children. No one knows
what happened to the rest. Does it matter
what date it is? It can be any date. The rain
will fall just as hard and death could not care.

Five children went into hiding. They searched
for the smallest place they could find.
They had experience playing *Hide and Seek*.
We heard Hans say the dogs found them
and tore them to pieces, but Hans
has a habit of saying it is raining
while standing in sunlight. We heard they survived,

but during war, such great news
is also misleading. Often, misleading
is how wars are started anyway.

Twelve of us children are transported to Vught
after Overijessel was declare cleansed
and fit for living. I could read the signpost.
A man was hung off it. I turned away
from looking directly at the bloated corpse
drawing flies. I changed directions
like a flower searches for light.

Now we are told to walk the rest of the way.
I know by the sun we are headed west.
They make us walk faster. We are almost running.
I hear a gunshot. One of the children
did not run fast enough.

One of the soldiers informs their leader
a place called Auschwitz is close.

    14.

We have not eaten in so long
we eat our nightmares.
We become thin as shadows at noon.
We count the xylophone of our ribs.
Some starved to death in their sleep.
Some never come back from work detail.
We cannot remember what day it is.
Someone has eaten a spider.

One of the soldiers informs the Commandant
they must move —
the enemy is near.

The leader does not like this information.
He shoots the messenger.

He points his gun towards the rest of us —
the few still panting. He counts the bullets
in his cylinder. He spins it, points, and clicks.

    15.

Who among us can say
this will never happen again?
The next time you see a stranger
remember you are a stranger too.

When you say some bad words
about a person you do not know,
remember they could be mumbling about you.

When you hear whispers,
listen how they say who does not belong here.
Remember they could say that about you.

    16.

At Auschwitz, the liberating soldiers who arrived
could not decide which bothered them more:

the mass graves;

the emaciated bodies;
the piles of empty children shoes.

There are people in this world
who deny this ever happened.
There are people who will say anything
to spread hate.

The best way to stop hate
is to not listen.

    17.

All wars are the same war.

INLAND WITH WATER

Kath Abela Wilson
FOR THE CHILDREN

gentle earth
the quiet day I pressed
against your green
and listened . . .
my pulse or yours

underwater
jigsaw
so busy
putting the pieces back together
the feet of swans

stroking the back
of deep green moss
yellow caterpillar
I press my pen
to a bark green page

watching the storm
scatter camellias
we hold on
to the inside
of our world

we carry the weight
of hidden nests
these thoughts
that play like wind
in our hair

Acknowledgments

Mara Buck
"Blood on the street"
Limited print edition in *Whirlwind #4*, Philadelphia, 5/15

Fern G.Z. Carr
"Lockdown – This Is Not a Drill"
Dirtcakes

Hedy Habra
"No Man's Land"
The Kerf

"To Amal"
Mizna Literary Journal

Lou Ella Hickman
"Vigil"
New Verse News, February 18, 2018.

Susan Fox
"Cradle Song for a Child of War: Gaza, 2014"
Persimmon Tree, fall/winter 2014

Connie Post
"Accessory After the Fact"
The Stray Branch Spring/Summer 2015

Amy Small-McKinney
"Open a Window"
Online at *Bullets into Bells, Poets & Citizens Respond to Gun Violence*, curated by Ellen McGrath Smith.

Margo Taft Stever
"Nothing's Holding up Nothing"

Connecticut Review. Also in the chapbook, *The Hudson Line,* Main Street Rag, 2012.

Maja Trochimczyk
"Standing Guard"
From *Slicing the Bread* by Finishing Line Press 2014

Contributor Notes

Margo Berdeshevsky, born in New York city, often writes and lives in Paris. *Before The Drought,* is her newest collection, (Glass Lyre Press, September 2017.) (In an early version, it was finalist for the National Poetry Series.) Berdeshevsky is author as well of *Between Soul & Stone,* and *But a Passage in Wilderness,* (Sheep Meadow Press.) Her book of illustrated stories, *Beautiful Soon Enough,* received the first Ronald Sukenick Innovative Fiction Award for Fiction Collective Two (University of Alabama Press.) Other honors include the Robert H. Winner Award from the Poetry Society of America, a portfolio of her poems in the *Aeolian Harp Anthology* #1 (Glass Lyre Press,) the *& Now Anthology of the Best of Innovative Writing,* and numerous Pushcart Prize nominations. Her works appear in the American journals: *Poetry International, New Letters, Kenyon Review, Plume, The Collagist, Tupelo Quarterly, Gulf Coast, Southern Humanities Review, Pleiades, Prairie Schooner, The American Journal of Poetry,* & *Jacar Press—One,* among many others. In Europe her works have been seen in *The Poetry Review* (UK), *Levure Littéraire, The Creative Process, The Wolf, Europe, Siècle 21,* & *Confluences Poétiques.* A multi genre hybrid of poems, *Square Black Key,* waits at the gate. She may be found reading from her books in London, Paris, New York City, or somewhere new in the world. Her *Letters from Paris* may be found in Poetry International, here: http://pionline.wordpress.com/category/letters-from-paris/ For more info kindly see: http://margoberdeshevsky.com

Carl Boon lives in Izmir, Turkey, where he teaches courses in American culture and literature at 9 Eylül University. His poems have appeared in many magazines, including *Posit, The Maine Review,* and *Diagram.* A Pushcart Prize nominee, Boon recently edited a volume on the sublime in American cultural studies.

Mara Buck writes and rants in a self-constructed hideaway in the Maine woods. Her story "TROPHY" just won the 2018 Scottish Arts Club Short Story Prize. Other recent first prizes include the F. Scott Fitzgerald Poetry Prize, the Binnacle Prize. Her work has also been awarded/short-listed by *Faulkner-Wisdom, Hackney, Balticon, Carpe Articulum,* and has been published in Hektoen International

Medical Journal, Huff Post, Crack the Spine, Blue Fifth, Pithead Chapel, Tishman, Whirlwind, etc. *and in numerous print anthologies. Current projects include the ubiquitous novel and a collection of strange stories of Maine.*

Fern G. Z. Carr is a former lawyer, teacher and past President of both the Society for the Prevention of Cruelty to Animals and Project Literacy Kelowna Society. A Full Member of and former Poet-in-Residence for the League of Canadian Poets, this Pushcart Prize nominee composes and translates poetry in six languages including Mandarin Chinese. Carr has been published extensively worldwide from Finland to Mauritius. Honours include having been cited as a contributor to the Prakalpana Literary Movement in India as well as having had her work taught at West Virginia University, set to music by a Juno-nominated musician, and featured online in *The Globe and Mail*, Canada's national newspaper. Her poem, "I Am", was chosen by the Parliamentary Poet Laureate as Poem of the Month for Canada. Carr's poetry collection, *Shards of Crystal*, was published in Fall 2018 by Silver Bow Publishing. She is thrilled to have one of her poems currently orbiting the planet Mars aboard NASA'S MAVEN spacecraft. www.ferngzcarr.com

Joan Colby has published widely in journals such as *Poetry, Atlanta Review, South Dakota Review, Gargoyle, Pinyon, Little Patuxent Review, Spillway, Midwestern Gothic* and others. Awards include two Illinois Arts Council Literary Awards and an Illinois Arts Council Fellowship in Literature. She has published 20 books including *Selected Poems* from FutureCycle Press which received the 2013 FutureCycle Prize and *Ribcage* from Glass Lyre Press which has been awarded the 2015 Kithara Book Prize. Three of her poems have been featured on *Verse Daily* and another is among the winners of the 2016 Atlanta Review International Poetry Contest. Her newest books are *Carnival* from FutureCycle Press, *The Seven Heavenly Virtues* from Kelsay Books and *Her Heartsongs* from Presa Press. Colby is a senior editor of FutureCycle Press and an associate editor of Good Works Review. Website: www.joancolby.com.

J. P. Dancing Bear is co-editor for *Verse Daily* and Dream Horse Press. He is the author of fourteen collections of poetry, most recently, *Cephalopodic* (Glass Lyre Press, 2015). His next book, *Fish Singing Foxes* will be released early in 2019 by Salmon Poetry, and his book, *Of Oracles and Monsters*, will be released by Glass Lyre Press also in 2019. His work has appeared or will shortly in *American Literary Review, Crazyhorse, the DIAGRAM* and elsewhere.

A former high school English teacher, **Carole Conner Davis's** writing has appeared in *The Whimsic Alley Book of Spells, The Innocence of Children, Wisdom of Our Mothers: Stories and poems by daughters and sons, Pawsitively Awesome Pet Poems, Best Modern Voices, Volume 1: A Poetry Anthology, The Language of Leadership, Trellis Magazine,* in products from Blue Mountain Arts, Inc., and on numerous web sites. Carole has regularly entered poetry contests, read at local poetry readings, and had an assortment of poetry, greeting cards, stories, essays and other writings published. She particularly enjoys parody and greeting card writing, reading, watching professional tennis, acting in local television and films, and handcrafting dance tiaras and jewelry.

Terri Kirby Erickson is the author of five full-length collections of award winning poetry. Her work has appeared or is forthcoming in *American Life in Poetry, Asheville Poetry Review, Atlanta Review, Connotation Press, storySouth, The Christian Century, The Writer's Almanac, Valparaiso Poetry Review, Verse Daily,* and many others. Awards include the Joy Harjo Poetry Prize, Nazim Hikmet Award, Atlanta Review International Publication Prize, and a Nautilus Silver Book Award. She lives in North Carolina.

Tikvah Feinstein's poetry is widely published in the USA and internationally, including *Verbal Art, Loyalhanna Review* and *Boston Poetry Magazine.* A graduate of the University of Pittsburgh, her writing career began when a story was published in its literary journal. Since then she has worked as staff writer for a daily newspaper, is author of 4 books, and has edited and illustrated others. Editor and publisher of *Taproot Literary Review* for 25 editions, her story "The Purpose of Tears" won the 2017 Westmoreland Short Story Award from Westmoreland Arts & Heritage Festival. She has been chosen by the Marquis Research Committee to receive the "Albert Nelson Marquis Lifetime Achievement Award" for 2019 for 30 years of professional accomplishments, and lasting contributions to the field of literature.

Mike Finley has been writing and performing for the Twin Cities scene for nearly 50 years. He has written over 200 books. His hallmarks are powerful storytelling, connecting with audiences, and having fun. Critic Michael Cuddihy wrote of Mike: "In no one else's work, except Vallejo's, do I sense such desire straining at the limits of words."

Susan Fox's poems have appeared in dozens of well-known literary and popular journals, from *Poetry* and *The Paris Review* and *The New York Quarterly* to *The New York Times*. She was born in Ohio and has lived in New York (where she taught English Literature in the City University), Rome, Paris, and rural Normandy. She's published literary criticism and travel journalism, an opera to her original full-length libretto about a hidden child in World War II had its semi-professional premiere in New York, and her screenplay of another Holocaust story was optioned for film. She lives now in Manhattan with her husband, physicist Steve Orenstein.

Diane Frank's new book of poems, *Canon for Bears and Ponderosa Pines*, was published in 2018 by Glass Lyre Press. She is editor of the bestselling anthology, *River of Earth and Sky: Poems for the 21st Century*, which is like a box of chocolate for poets. She lives in San Francisco, where she dances, plays cello, and creates her life as an art form. Her Nepal memoir, *Letters from a Sacred Mountain Place: A Journey through the Nepal Himalayas* was published in 2018 by Nirala Publications, with stories, poems and 53 color photographs.

Marc Frazier has widely published poetry in journals including *The Spoon River Poetry Review, ACM, Good Men Project, f(r)iction, The Gay and Lesbian Review, Slant, Permafrost, Plainsongs,* and *Poet Lore*. He has had memoir from his book *WITHOUT* published in *Gravel, The Good Men Project, decomP, Autre, Cobalt Magazine, Evening Street Review,* and *Punctuate*. Marc, an LGBTQ+ writer, is the recipient of an Illinois Arts Council Award for poetry, has been featured on *Verse Daily*, and has been nominated for a Pushcart Prize and a "best of the net." His book *The Way Here* and his two chapbooks are available on Amazon as well as his second full-length collection titled *Each Thing Touches* (Glass Lyre Press). *Willingly*, his third poetry book, will be published by Adelaide Books in 2019. His website is www.marcfrazier.org

Jessica Goody's debut poetry collection *Defense Mechanisms* (Phosphene Publishing, 2016) was chosen as a "Power Read" by *The Hilton Head Monthly* and a Book of the Month by *The Creativity Webzine*. Her second collection, *Phoenix*, will be released by WordTech Communications in March 2019. Jessica's writing has appeared in over three dozen publications, including *The Wallace Stevens Journal*. A columnist for *SunSations Magazine*, she was the winner of the 2016 Magnets and Ladders Poetry Prize.

Hedy Habra has authored two poetry collections, *Under Brushstrokes,* finalist for the USA Best Book Award and the International Poetry Book Award, and *Tea in Heliopolis,* winner of the USA Best Book Award and finalist for the International Poetry Book Award. Her story collection, *Flying Carpets,* won the Arab American National Book Award's Honorable Mention and was finalist for the Eric Hoffer Award. A twelve-time nominee for the Pushcart Prize and Best of the Net, her work appears in *Cimarron Review, The Bitter Oleander, Blue Fifth Review, Cider Press Review, Drunken Boat, Gargoyle, Nimrod, Poet Lore, World Literature Today* and *Verse Daily*. Her website is hedyhabra.com

Vernita Hall is the author of *Where William Walked: Poems About Philadelphia and Its People of Color* (Willow Books, 2018), winner of the Willow Books Grand Prize for Poetry and of the Robert Creeley Prize from Marsh Hawk Press, and *The Hitchhiking Robot Learns About Philadelphians* (Moonstone Press, 2017), winner of the Moonstone Chapbook Contest. Her poems and essays appear or are forthcoming in numerous journals and anthologies. A lifelong Philadelphian, Hall holds an MFA in Creative Writing from Rosemont College and serves on the poetry review board of *Philadelphia Stories.*

Sister Lou Ella Hickman is a former teacher and librarian. She is a certified spiritual director as well as a poet and writer. Her poems have appeared in numerous magazines such as *America, First Things, Emmanuel, Third Wednesday,* and *new verse news*. Her first book of poetry entitled *she: robed and wordless* was published in 2015 by Press 53.

Lois P. Jones has work published or forthcoming in several anthologies including *New Voices: Contemporary Writers Confronting the Holocaust* (Vallentine Mitchell of London (2019); *The Poet's Quest for God* (Eyewear Publishing), and *Wide Awake: Poetry of Los Angeles and Beyond* (The Pacific Coast Poetry Series). Other publications include *Narrative, American Poetry Journal, One, Tupelo Quarterly, The Warwick Review, Cider Press Review, Terrain* and *Tinderbox Poetry Journal.* Honors include the Lascaux Poetry Prize in 2017, the Bristol Poetry Prize in 2016 and the Tiferet Poetry Prize in 2012 with work shortlisted for the Bridport Prize in poetry in 2016 and 2017. She hosts KPFK's *Poets Café* in Los Angeles and co-hosts the long running Moonday Poetry Series at the Flintridge Bookstore. Lois is the poetry editor for the Utne and Pushcart Prize winning *Kyoto Journal* - a quarterly publication that transcends place, while respecting and celebrating regional and local identity. Jones' first collection of poems, *Night Ladder*, is Glass Lyre Press's 2017 Editor's Choice and listed for the Julie Suk Award.

Allison Joseph lives in Carbondale, Illinois, where she is Professor of English and Director of the MFA Program in Creative Writing at Southern Illinois University. She serves as poetry editor of *Crab Orchard Review*. Her books and chapbooks include *What Keeps Us Here* (Ampersand Press), *Soul Train* (Carnegie Mellon University Press), *In Every Seam* (University of Pittsburgh Press), *Worldly Pleasures* (Word Tech Communications), *Imitation of Life* (Carnegie Mellon UP), *Voice: Poems* (Mayapple Press), *My Father's Kites* (Steel Toe Books), *Trace Particles* (Backbone Press), *Little Epiphanies* (NightBallet Press), *Mercurial* (Mayapple Press), *Mortal Rewards* (White Violet Press), *Multitudes* (Word Poetry), *The Purpose of Hands* (Glass Lyre Press), *Double Identity* (Singing Bone Press) *Corporal Muse* (Sibling Rivalry) and *What Once You Loved* (Barefoot Muse Press). Her most recent full-length collection, *Confessions of a Barefaced Woman* was published by Red Hen Press in June 2018. She is the literary partner and wife of poet and editor Jon Tribble.

Laura M Kaminski (Halima Ayuba) grew up in Nigeria, went to school in New Orleans, and currently lives in rural Missouri. She is the author of several poetry collections and chapbooks, most recently *The Heretic's Hymnal: 99 New and Selected Poems* (Babylon Books / Balkan Press, 2018).

Catherine Keefe is a California poet, essayist, social justice activist, and 2017 Pushcart Prize nominee. Recent work appeared in *TAB: The Journal of Poetry and Poetics, The Gettysburg Review;* and the anthologies *Forgotten Women: A Tribute in Poetry (Grayson Books, 2017)* and *Thirty Days: The Best of Tupelo Press 30/30 Project's First Year* (2015). Catherine is a member of the Orange County Human Relations Commission Anti-Hate Speakers Assembly which offers anti-hate presentations to the local community.

Chris 'Irish Goat' Knodel is an author, poet, and ultra-distance runner in San Antonio, TX. He currently holds a BA in History, an MA in History/Art History, an MA in English Literature & Rhetoric, an MFA in Creative Writing, and an MS in Publishing. His poetry and short fiction have been featured in/by *Alba, Allegro Poetry Magazine, Asses of Parnassus, DreamFusion Press, Ealain, Four Parts Press, Glass Lyre Press, Grey Wolfe Publishing, Haiku Journal, Highfield Press, Icarus Down Review, Kind of a Hurricane Press, Pretty Owl Poetry, Tanka Journal, The Wolfian, The*

Write Place at the Write Time, Writer's Quibble, Yellow Chair Review, Ygdrasil, Zimbell House Publishing, Zodiac Review & *Zombie Logic Review.* He can be easily spotted by his kilt, tattoos and six inch, flaming-red, Van Dyke goatee.

Rustin Larson's poetry has appeared in *The New Yorker, The Iowa Review, North American Review, Poetry East,* and *The American Entomologist Poet's Guide to the Orders of Insects.* He is the author of *The Wine-Dark House* (Blue Light Press, 2009), *Crazy Star* (selected for the Loess Hills Book's Poetry Series in 2005), *Bum Cantos, Winter Jazz, & The Collected Discography of Morning,* winner of the 2013 Blue Light Book Award (Blue Light Press, San Francisco), *The Philosopher Savant* (Glass Lyre Press, 2015) and *Pavement,* winner of the Blue Light Poetry Prize for 2016.

Lyn Lifshin has published over 130 books and chapbooks including 3 from Black Sparrow Press: *Cold Comfort, Before It's Light and Another Woman Who Looks Like Me.* Before *Secretariat: The Red Freak, The Miracle,* Lifshin published her prize winning book about the short lived beautiful race horse Ruffian, *The Licorice Daughter: My Year With Ruffian* and *Barbaro: Beyond Brokenness.* Recent books include *Ballroom, All the Poets Who Have Touched Me, Living and Dead. All True, Especially The Lies, Light At the End: The Jesus Poems, Katrina, Mirrors, Persphone, Lost In The Fog, Knife Edge* & *Absinthe: The Tango Poems* . NYQ books published *A Girl Goes into The Woods.* Also just out: *For the Roses* poems after Joni Mitchell and *Hitchcock Hotel* from Danse Macabre. *Secretariat: The Red Freak, The Miracle.* And *Tangled as the Alphabet,*— *The Istanbul Poems* from NightBallet Press Just released as well *Malala,* the dvd of *Lyn Lifshin: Not Made of Glass. The Marilyn Poems* was just released from Rubber Boots Press. An update to her Gale Research Autobiography is out: *Lips, Blues, Blue Lace: On The Outside.* Also just out is a dvd of the documentary film about her: *Lyn Lifshin: Not Made Of Glass.* Just out: *Femme Eterna* and *Moving Through Stained Glass: the Maple Poems.* just out: *Degas Little Dancer* and *Winter Poems* from Kind of a Hurricane press, *Paintings and Poems,* from Tangerine press (just out) and *The Silk Road* from Night Ballet, *alivelikealoadedgun* from Transcendent Zero Press.

Alison Luterman's three books of poetry are *The Largest Possible Life; See How We Almost Fly;* and *Desire Zoo.* Her poems and stories have appeared in *The Sun, Rattle, Salon, Prairie Schooner, Nimrod, The Atlanta Review, Tattoo Highway,* and elsewhere. Her poetry is often used by therapists, coaches, and meditation teachers. She has also written an e-book of personal essays, *Feral*

City, and more than half a dozen plays, including *Oasis, Saying Kaddish With My Sister, Glitter and Spew, Touched*, and two musicals, *The Chain* and *Nasty Women*.

Alison performs with the Oakland-based improvisation troupe Wing It! and has given writing workshops all over the country, including at Omega and Esalen Institutes. She teaches memoir at The Writing Salon in Berkeley, and is available for private coaching in writing or creativity, both in-person or on-line. She also loves to teach easy accessible theater games and writing prompts to groups of all kinds. For more information, please visit her website at www.alisonluterman.net.

Dennis Maloney is a poet and translator. A number of volumes of his own poetry have been published including *The Map Is Not the Territory: Poems & Translations and Just Enough*. His book *Listening to Tao Yuan Ming* was published by Glass Lyre Press in 2015. A bilingual German/English, *Empty Cup* was published in Germany in 2017. *The Things I Notice Now* is forthcoming from MadHat Press in fall 2018. He is also the editor and publisher of the widely respected White Pine Press in Buffalo, NY, and divides his time between Buffalo, NY and Big Sur, CA.

Catherine McGuire is a writer and artist with a deep concern for our planet's future. She has four decades of published poetry, four poetry chapbooks, a full-length poetry book, *Elegy for the 21st Century* (FutureCycle Press) and a deindustrial science fiction novel *Lifeline* (Founders House Publishing). Find her at www.cathymcguire.com.

Ken Meisel is a poet and psychotherapist from the Detroit area. He is a 2012 Kresge Arts Literary Fellow, Pushcart Prize nominee, Swan Duckling chapbook contest winner, winner of the Liakoura Prize and the author of seven poetry collections: *Mortal Lullabies* (FutureCycle Press: 2018), *The Drunken Sweetheart at My Door* (FutureCycle Press: 2015), *Scrap Metal Mantra Poems*(Main Street Rag: 2013), *Beautiful Rust* (Bottom Dog Press: 2009), *Just Listening* (Pure Heart Press: 2007), *Before Exiting* (Pure Heart Press: 2006) and *Sometimes the Wind* (March Street Press: 2002). His work in over 100 national magazines including *Cream City Review, Rattle, Dressing Room Poetry Journal, Midwestern Gothic, Concho River Review, San Pedro River Review, Boxcar Review, Origins Journal, The Bookends Review, Muddy River Poetry Review, Pirene's Fountain, Lake Effect, Soundings East, Gravel Magazine*, and *Lullwater*. He was the featured poet interview in *Rattle* Magazine's September, 2017 Rust Belt Issue.

Megan Merchant is an editor at *The Comstock Review*. Her most recent book, *Grief Flowers* (Glass Lyre Press) is out in the world. You can find her work at meganmerchant.wix.com/poet.

Marsha Warren Mittman's humorous memoir, *You Know You Moved to South Dakota from New York City WHEN...* is forthcoming from Scurfpea Publishing. Her poetry, essays, and short stories have been published in American, British, and German literary journals, magazines, and anthologies. Recently: *Pure Slush*, *The Wild Word* (Berlin), *Oakwood*, *Rat's Ass Review*, *Novelty* (London), *In-flight*, *Porcupine*, and a sixth *Chicken Soup for the Soul* tale. Select poems from *Patriarchal Chronicles: Women's Worldwide Tears* are currently being crafted into a staged production. She's the recipient of thirteen writing distinctions in the States and Ireland.

Cameron Morse lives with his wife Lili and son Theodore in Blue Springs, Missouri. He was diagnosed with a glioblastoma in 2014. With a 14.6 month life expectancy, he entered the Creative Writing program at the University of Missouri—Kansas City and, in 2018, graduated with an M.F.A. His poems have been published in over 100 different magazines, including *New Letters*, *Bridge Eight*, and *South Dakota Review*. His first collection, *Fall Risk*, won Glass Lyre Press's 2018 Best Book Award. His second, *Father Me Again*, is forthcoming from Spartan Press.

Travis Mossotti was awarded the 2011 May Swenson Poetry Award for his first collection of poems *About the Dead* (USU Press, 2011), and his second collection *Field Study* won the 2013 Melissa Lanitis Gregory Poetry Prize (Bona Fide Books, 2014). His third collection *Narcissus Americana* was selected by Billy Collins as the winner of the 2018 Miller Williams Prize (University of Arkansas Press, 2018). Mossotti has also published two chapbooks, and recent poems of his have appeared in issues of the *EPOCH*, *Columbia Poetry Review*, *Natural Bridge*, and elsewhere. He was a 2015 Regional Arts Commission Artist Fellow and was also a featured presenter at the TEDxGatewayArch in 2016. Mossotti teaches in the writing program at Webster University and works as a System Engineer II for the Research Management System at Washington University. In 2018 Mossotti was named a Biodiversity Fellow at the Living Earth Collaborative at Washington University, and he has served as Poet-in-Residence at the Endangered Wolf Center in St. Louis since 2012.

Robbi Nester is the author of three books of poems: a chapbook, *Balance* (White Violet, 2012), and two full collections—*A Likely Story* (Moon Tide, 2014) and *Other-Wise* (Kelsay, 2017). She has also edited two anthologies of poetry: *The Liberal Media Made Me Do It!* (Nine Toes, 2014) and an Ekphrastic e-book, *Over the Moon: Birds, Beasts, and Trees*—celebrating the photography of Beth Moon. Her poetry, reviews, essays, and articles have appeared widely. Her collection *Narrow Bridge* will be available in the new year from Main Street Rag.

Aimee Nezhukumatathil is the author of four books of poetry, most recently, *Oceanic* (Copper Canyon, 2018). With Ross Gay, she co-authored the chapbook, *Lace & Pyrite: Letters from Two Gardens*. Her collection of nature essays is forthcoming from Milkweed. Honors include a Pushcart Prize and a fellowship from the National Endowment for the Arts. She is poetry editor of *Orion* magazine and professor of English in The University of Mississippi's MFA program.

Connie Post served as Poet Laureate of Livermore, California (2005 to 2009). Her work has appeared dozens of journals, including *Calyx, Aurorean, Atticus Review, Comstock Review, Cold Mountain Review Slipstream, River Styx, Spoon River Poetry Review, Two Bridges Review, Valparaiso Poetry Review* and *Verse Daily*. Her Chapbook *And when the Sun Drops* won the Aurorean's Editor's choice award in 2013. She has been short listed for the Jack Kerouac Poetry Prize, The Muriel Craft Bailey awards (*Comstock Review*) Lois Cranston Memorial Awards (*Calyx*), and Gary Gildner Award (*I 70 Review*). Her first full length book, *Floodwater* (Glass Lyre Press 2014) won the Lyrebird Award. Her awards include the 2017 Prick of the Spindle Poetry Competition, the Caesura Award and the 2016 Crab Creek Poetry Award

George Jisho Robertson is 84 years old this year. He is a passionate gardener, photographer and poet. He has three daughters and five grandchildren. He has lived in a small apartment in Peckham, London, UK since 1999 (the first settled home he ever had). In a busy urban area he has created a wild life sanctuary and woodland garden stocked with native plants and plants from all over the world–a garden alive with birdsong, fragrance, colour and form. The garden is a great support for the elders who live in the apartment block, providing beauty interest and entertainment. From 1959 he worked in State education for 33 years, becoming a Senior High School Principal at the age of 36 and continued, managing three schools until he retired in 1989 to train as a Zen priest. In that role for a year he became the Principal of a Day Care Center for the children of Black and Hispanic single mothers who came through Rehab and/or long-term unemployment, as did the teaching staff, in one of the toughest cities in New York State, namely Yonkers (also known as Crack City.) "Since he arrived in Peckham he has devoted his life to his family, neighbours and friends–his closest friend and he have known one another for 44 years. His photographs and poems can be visited on his Facebook page–go to george jisho robertson.

Michael Rothenberg is editor of BigBridge.org and co-founder of 100 Thousand Poets for Change. His most recent books of poetry include *Drawing The Shade* (Dos Madres Press, 2016), *Wake Up and Dream* (MadHat Press, 2017), and a bi-lingual edition of *Indefinite Detention: A Dog Story* (Varasek Ediciones, Madrid, Spain, 2017). A bi-lingual edition of the poetic journals *Tally Ho and the Cowboy Dream/The Real and False Journals: Book 5* is due out from Varasek Ediciones Madrid, Spain in Spring 2019. He lives in Tallahassee, Florida where he is FSU Libraries Poet in Residence.

Neil Silberblatt's poems have appeared, or will soon appear, in numerous journals, including *The American Journal of Poetry, Tikkun, Poetica Magazine, The Aurorean, Mom Egg Review, Ibbetson Street Press, Naugatuck River Review, Chantarelle's Notebook, Canopic Jar, Muddy River Poetry Review, Nixes Mate Review,* and *The Good Men Project.* His work has also selected for various anthologies, including University of Connecticut's *Teacher-Writer* magazine; and *Culinary Poems* (Pirene's Fountain). He has published two poetry collections: *So Far, So Good* (2012), and *Present Tense* (2013), and has been nominated for a Pushcart Prize. His most recent poetry book, *Past Imperfect* (Nixes Mate Books, 2018), has been nominated for the Mass. Book Award in Poetry. Neil is the founder/director of Voices of Poetry which has organized and presented a series of poetry events (featuring acclaimed poets) at various venues in NY, NJ, CT and MA, including The Mount / Edith Wharton's home in Lenox, MA, and The Rubin Museum of Art in NYC.

Kalpna Singh-Chitnis is an Indo-American poet, writer, actor and filmmaker. She received a masters degree in Political Science from Magadh University, Bodhgaya, and studied film directing at the New York Film Academy in Hollywood. She taught Political Science and International Relations to postgraduate students in India, before moving to the United States in 1994. Author of *Bare Soul*, the winner of the 2017 Naji Naaman Literary Prize for Poetry and three collections of poems in Hindi, she won the prestigious Bihar Rajbhasha Award given by the government of Bihar, India, for her first poetry collection *Chand Ka Paivand* (Patch of Moon), before she was twenty one; and was given the title of Bihar Shri (Jewel of Bihar) in 1988. She also received the Rajiv Gandhi Global Excellence Award in 2014 for her contributions to literature and cinema, and was nominated for "Honor of Yeast Litteraire" by *Levure Litterarie* magazine in Paris, France. Kalpna's work has been widely published and translated into many languages. Her English poetry collection, *Bare Soul* has been translated into Arabic by poet and translator Nizar Sartawi. She is also the creator and editor of *Life and Legends* literary journal. More about Kalpna Singh-Chitnis at www.kalpnasinghchitnis.com

Amy Small-McKinney won The Kithara Book Prize 2016 (Glass Lyre Press) for her second full-length collection of poems, *Walking Toward Cranes*. Her poems appeared in *Connotation Press: An Online Artifact, American Poetry Review, The Cortland Review, Construction, LIPS, Tiferet Journal*, and elsewhere, and are forthcoming in *The Indianapolis Review*. Small-McKinney's poems also appear in *Veils, Halos, and Shackles: International Poetry on the Abuse and Oppression of Women* (eds Charles Fishman & Smita Sahay), and *BARED: Contemporary Poetry and Art on Bras and Breasts* (ed. Laura Madeline Wiseman). Her work has been translated into Korean in *Bridging The Waters II* (CrossCultural Communications). January 2018, she traveled to Ireland with the Drew University MFA in Poetry program where she participated on the panel, Kindred Spirits, at the Transatlantic Connections Conference.

LeRoy Sorenson has published or will publish poems in such journals as *The American Journal of Poetry, The Cider Press Review, Crab Orchard Review, Dr. T. J. Eckleburg Review, Naugatuck River Review, Nimrod International Journal of Prose and Poetry, Pirene's Fountain, Sow's Ear* and other journals. Main Street Rag published his first book of poetry, *Forty Miles North of Nowhere*, in early 2016. He was a participant in the Loft's Mentor program and a graduate of the Loft's Foreword program.

Margo Taft Stever's full-length collection, *CRACKED PIANO*, will be published by CavanKerry Press in 2019. Her four poetry collections include *The Lunatic Ball*, Kattywompus Press, 2015; *The Hudson Line*, Main Street Rag, 2012; *Frozen Spring*, winner of the Mid-List Press First Series Award for Poetry, 2002; and *Reading the Night Sky*, winner of the 1996 Riverstone Poetry Chapbook Competition. She co-authored *Looking East: William Howard Taft and the 1905 U.S. Diplomatic Mission to Asia* (Zhejiang University Press, 2012) and Orange

Frazier Press (2015), a collaboration between University of Cincinnati and Zhejiang University Press. The Chinese-language version was published by Zhejiang University in 2012. Her poems, essays, and reviews have appeared in magazines and anthologies including *upstreet, Blackbird, Salamander; Poem-A-Day,* The Academy of American Poets, *Cincinnati Review, Salamander, Prairie Schooner, New England Review, Connecticut Review, Poet Lore, West Branch, Seattle Review,* and *No More Masks* (first edition). She is the founder of The Hudson Valley Writers Center and the founding and current co-editor of Slapering Hol Press. For more information, please see: www.margostever.com.

Ambika Talwar is an educator, poet and artist, who has composed poems since her teen years. She has authored and self-published *Creative Resonance: Poetry—Elegant Play, Elegant Change; 4 Stars & 25 Roses* (poems for her father) and, recently, *My Greece: Mirrors & Metamorphoses,* a poetic biographical spiritual journey through Greece. Ambika's poems appear in *CQ* and *Grateful Conversations* both published in 2018. Her earlier poems are in *Kyoto Journal; Inkwater Ink, vol. 3; Chopin with Cherries, On Divine Names; VIA, Poets on Site collections, Tower Journal, St. Julian's Press, Life & Legends, YTJ* and others. Her ecstatic writing style makes her poetry a "bridge to other worlds." Ambika affirms it is creativity that awakens us and makes us activators of change. Interviewed by *Poets' Café* on KPFK, she earned Best Original Story Award at a film festival in Belgium for her short *Androgyne* in 2000. A wellness practitioner using energetic processes for full spectrum healing, she lives in Los Angeles/New Delhi and has taught English at Cypress College, California for several years. Sites: www.creativeinfinities.com, www.goldenmatrixvisions.com

Susan Tepper is the author of six published books of fiction and poetry. 'Boys' is a poem from her newest collection-in-progress titled *THE WAR BOOK.* Tepper lives with her husband and her dog Otis in the NY area. A twenty year writer, she is the recipient of many awards. www.susantepper.com

Jon Tribble's newest collection of poems, *God of the Kitchen* from Glass Lyre Press, is about the experiences and culture of working at Kentucky Fried Chicken as a teenager in the late 1970s. He is also the author of *Natural State* (Glass Lyre Press, 2016.) and *And There Is Many a Good Thing* (Salmon Poetry, 2017). His poems have appeared in print journals and anthologies, including *Ploughshares, Poetry, Crazyhorse, Quarterly West,* and *The Jazz Poetry Anthology,* and online at *storySouth, The Blue Mountain Review,* and *Vox Populi.* He teaches at Southern Illinois University Carbondale, where he is the managing editor of *Crab Orchard Review* and the series editor of the Crab Orchard Series in Poetry published by SIU Press.

Maja Trochimczyk, Ph.D., is a Polish American poet, music historian, photographer, and author of seven books of poetry, including *Miriam's Iris* (2008), *Slicing the Bread* (2014), *The Rainy Bread* (2016), *Into Light* (2016), and two anthologies, *Chopin with Cherries* (2010) and *Meditations on Divine Names* (2012). Hundreds of her poems appeared in such journals as the *California Quarterly, Cosmopolitan Review, Ekphrasis Journal, Epiphany Magazine, Lily Literary Review, Loch Raven Review, Lummox Journal, Quill and Parchment, Pirene's Fountain, Poezja Dzisiaj, The Scream Online, Spectrum* and anthologies by Poets on Site, Southern California Haiku Study Group, and others. As a Polish music historian, she published seven books, most recently *Górecki in Context: Essays on Music (2017)* and *Frédéric Chopin: A Research and Information Guide (rev. ed., 2015)*. A former Poet Laureate of Sunland-Tujunga, she is the founder of Moonrise Press, and Board Secretary of the Polish American Historical Association. Her research studies, articles and book chapters appeared in English, Polish, and in translations in ten countries. She read papers at over 80 international conferences and is a recipient of honors and awards from Polish, Canadian, and American institutions, such as the American Council of Learned Societies, the Polish Ministry of Culture, PAHA, McGill University, and the University of Southern California. www.trochimczyk.net

Robert Walton is a retired middle school teacher and a lifelong rock climber with many ascents in the Sierras and Pinnacles National Park. His writing about climbing has appeared in the Sierra Club's *Ascent*. His publishing credits include works of science fiction, fantasy and poetry. He also worked as a newspaper columnist for a time. His historical novel *Dawn Drums* won the 2014 New Mexico Book Awards Tony Hillerman Prize for best fiction, first place in the 2014 Arizona Authors competition and first place in the historical fiction category of the 2017 Readers Choice Awards. Most recently, his short story "Uriah" was published in *Assisi*, a literary journal associated with St. Francis College in Brooklyn.

Martin Willitts Jr. is a poetry editor for *Comstock Review*. He won the 2014 Dylan Thomas International Poetry Award; *Rattle* Ekphrastic Challenge, and Stephen A. DiBiase Poetry Prize, 2018. He won a Central New York Individual Artist Award and provided *Poetry On The Bus* which had 48 poems in local buses including 20 bi-lingual poems from 7 different languages. He has 23 chapbooks including the winner of the Turtle Island Quarterly Editor's Choice Award, *The Wire Fence Holding Back the World* (Flowstone Press, 2017), plus 14 full-length collections including *The Uncertain Lover* (Dos Madres Press, 2018), and *Home Coming Celebration* (FutureCycle Press, 2019).

Kath Abela Wilson lived and wrote mainly in Santa Barbara, California for 30 years, and still maintains a residence there, where the Ocean infuses her poetry with salty enigmatic inspiration. She lived for years on a street that led to stairs to the sea and walked there every day. Her poems and art are intimately linked with the tides, waves, stones and driftwood. Her free verse, and Asian short form poetry is published in hundreds of journals worldwide. She travels the world with her husband Rick, a math professor and historical and world flute collector and player, performing together. She hosts poetry meetings and salons at her home, and local gardens and museums. Recently her haiku was honored with third place in The Santoka International Haiku Contest, 2017 "Peace", and honorable mention in the Yuki Teikei Haiku Society Haiku Contest, 2017, and British Haiku Society Contest, 2017. Her tanka won first place in English language Tanka in the Fujisan Contest, 2017. She is secretary of the Tanka Society of America. Her chapbooks *Driftwood Monster, Haiku for Troubled Times* and *The Owl Still Asking, Tanka for Troubled Times* are available from Lulu, published by Moria Press, Locfo Chaps 2017.

Glass Lyre Press

exceptional works to replenish the spirit

Glass Lyre Press is an independent literary publisher interested in technically accomplished, stylistically distinct, and original work. Glass Lyre seeks diverse writers that possess a dynamic aesthetic and an ability to emotionally and intellectually engage a wide audience of readers.

Glass Lyre's vision is to connect the world through language and art. We hope to expand the scope of poetry and short fiction for the general reader through exceptionally well-written books, which evoke emotion, provide insight, and resonate with the human spirit.

Poetry Collections
Poetry Chapbooks
Select Short & Flash Fiction
Anthologies

www.GlassLyrePress.com

www.ingramcontent.com/pod-product-compliance
Lightning Source LLC
Chambersburg PA
CBHW020142130526
44591CB00030B/177